Tombstone

Tombstone

MYTH AND REALITY

—⌁—

Odie B. Faulk

New York
OXFORD UNIVERSITY PRESS
1972

978

Arizona – History
U.S. – The West – Hist

FOR THE ONE WHO READ IT FIRST
For reasons we both understand

Preface

The bad guys ride black horses and wear black hats—cattle rustlers, whiskey peddlers, horse thieves, unscrupulous Indian agents, stage robbers, Army deserters. The good guys ride white horses and wear white hats—sheriffs, deputies, town marshals, Wells, Fargo men, U. S. Marshals. The two sides each have their followers in the form of gang and posse, and they clash with gunfights at high noon, shootouts in the streets, and men ordered to leave town before sundown. All this transpires while the rest of the population sits in a nearby bar, apparently with nothing to do but drink, gamble, and witness the violence. A lawless, restless, brawling, fighting, eye-gouging, ear-biting breed, each with gun hanging low on hip, holster tied securely to thigh, ready to draw and fire with incredible speed and accuracy.

Such is the myth of the Tombstone of 1879-83, engendered by a plethora of pulp magazines and paperback novels and by telefilms and movies. It has been remarked facetiously that an intellectual is a man who can hear the "William Tell Overture" and not think of the Lone Ranger; that might equally read that an intellectual is a man who can hear the words "OK Corral" and not think of Tombstone—and Wyatt Earp. He has become a stock character in that American form of the medieval morality play, the western, a man who enlivened so many Saturday afternoons as we watched the matinee feature. Yet in the morass of fiction about Tombstone, of error, of deliberate lies, the reality of the town has been lost.

Tombstone in its heyday was largely male in population, principally young men without the restraints of wives, mothers, and sweethearts. They worked hard, most of them company employees laboring the standard ten-hour shift below ground six days a week. And then they played hard, drinking, watching girlie shows at the theaters, wenching with the "soiled doves" of the local "hog ranches," or else playing cards and talking endlessly of mines and mining. And there were some men in town who worked to build schools, churches, libraries, and other refinements of civilization; there were men who formed volunteer fire-fighting companies and literary societies; and there were some interested in amateur theatricals, music, and the arts—just as there were a few trying to get rich from the fruit of other men's labor. The weary miner coming home from town, perhaps a little drunk, who decided to steal a cat and thereby get a good night's sleep unmolested by the large number of rats infesting his shack is more typical of Tombstone in its glory days than is Wyatt Earp. He is the reality of the town.

This book, then, is an attempt to tell the story of Tombstone: how the mines were discovered, how the town grew, how the miners lived, why the boom ended and the mines closed, how the local citizens deliberately made theirs "the town too tough to die," and even the hows and whys of the violence that has become the Tombstone of national myth. There can be no answer to the question of why the Tombstone of myth has prevailed over the Tombstone of reality in the American consciousness. Perhaps a psychologist can supply that answer—the historian cannot.

In writing this book I have become increasingly indebted to several individuals and institutions. I first began work on Tombstone's history in 1964 through a research grant from the Arizona Historical Foundation; for that I thank its executive director, Bert Fireman, as well as for his guidance over these past seven years. Many of the materials for the book were secured by the staff of the Library at Oklahoma State University, to whom I am deeply grateful, while a grant from the Research Foundation at Oklahoma State University enabled me to secure yet other portions of it. Charles Colley and Margaret Sparks of the Arizona Historical Society in Tucson greatly aided me in my rambles through their excellent holdings; I honestly believe that no book on Arizona history could be written without the help of this institution. I also note with gratitude the courtesies extended me in years past by the staff of the Special Collections Division of the University of Arizona Library. And Don Bufkin of Tucson as always has been most helpful, supplying the information for the maps in this book.

Two last debts I here acknowledge: as always I owe much to the fine editorial staff of Oxford University Press, particularly Mr. Sheldon Meyer; and my deepest gratitude goes to the one to whom the book is dedicated, for without your patience, your counsel, and your willingness to listen the book would never have been completed.

ODIE B. FAULK

Stillwater, Oklahoma
December 1, 1971

Contents

xi

Tombstone

Introduction

Southeastern Arizona is a spectacular area. In its clear, dry air the mountains appear two-dimensional, like giant cardboard cutouts, seemingly placed here and there with no apparent order. Only when viewed from the air do they assume three-dimensional proportions; from this vantage point can be seen the creek beds and arroyos which lace their sides with wrinkles of age. Four sets of these sentinels guard the district that would become Tombstone: the Dragoon Mountains to the northeast, the Mule Mountains to the southeast, the Huachucas to the southwest, and the Whetstones to the northwest. These are strung out in the uncertain order of glaciers now melted, winds long dead, and rains eons since a part of the ocean. Rivulets, some called creeks, some mislabeled rivers, meander east and west from the mountains, dropping from the heights down across rolling hills and flat table lands to form an alluvial plain and to feed the main artery of the valley, the San Pedro River.

This stream, if in the eastern part of the United States, would hardly qualify as a good creek, but to the pioneers of the arid Southwest it was a river. It has its origins in Sonora, Mexico, in the Sierra Madre Occidental at a point from whence it drew its name, the Casa de San Pedro. Entering Arizona near longitude 110°, it flows northward to feed the Gila River, which in turn moves west to join the Colorado at Yuma Crossing, and thence runs southward to become part of the fabled Gulf of California. In its journey northward toward the Gila, the San Pedro at places drops rapidly in altitude, causing it to flow only some ten feet wide and thus to have steep banks of considerable depth; at other places it is broad and placid, a stately stream used for irrigation.

In the past fifty years man has changed the face of the San Pedro Valley. He has scraped off the natural vegetation—a rich variety of desert plants—to plant nutritious grass for cattle or else to locate crops considered more beneficial to humans. He has dug canals to distribute the water, built dams to store it, and perforated the earth with wells to secure yet more of it. He has built roads in a crazy patchwork quilt. And he has dotted the region with cattle, supplanting in large measure the original animals who roamed the area: deer, antelope, wild hogs, and rabbits, along with rattle-snakes, gila monsters, scorpions, and a multitude of black widow spiders. Even beaver once were trapped along the San Pedro's banks by bearded mountain men. Despite these changes which man has wrought, however, the land remains what it was originally —a hostile environment, a majestic beauty, and a rich opportunity.

This is the region that originally was the homeland of the Sobai-puri Indians. Linguistically and culturally a part of the Pima tribe, the Sobaipuris were a primitive people who had advanced little beyond the hunting and gathering stage when they were forced to merge with the Papagos by the encroachments of the more warlike Apaches in the eighteenth century. The Apaches, part of the great Athapascan linguistic group, had begun their migrations into the Southwest centuries before; those who settled in the San Pedro Valley were a sub-tribe known as the Chiricahua Apaches. They lived in brush shelters, called wickiups, borrowed enough from the Pueblo tribes to the north and east to weave baskets and to make pottery, and even did some farming. What most distinguished them from other desert tribes in the vicinity, however, was their ferocity as warriors. Perhaps because they felt threatened by those Indians they had dispossessed when they moved into the region, the Apaches became remorseless warriors and guerrilla fighters. Inhabitants of a hard land, they became, like it, hard. They were cruel to all other people. In fact, their economy, beyond some hunting and gathering, was based on booty gathered in raids.

For the Sobaipuri, the Pima, the Papago, and the Apache, life was not altogether a bleak, brutish existence of killing or being killed, raiding or being raided, however. There was the pleasure of the hunt, the providence of natural bounty, and the satisfaction of what they discerned to be the geographic beauty of their homeland. Yet their life was uncertain when game grew scarce, when crops failed, or when battles went against them. They suffered from disease, from periodic famine, and from man's inhumanity to man. Yet such was the only life they had ever known, and they doubtless found reason within it for hope, for laughter, for dreams.

The years of sole Indian hegemony in the valley of the San Pedro ended very inauspiciously. In the late spring of 1539, probably in May of that year, a Spanish Franciscan missionary, Fray Marcos de Niza, accompanied by Indians from the south and guided by a Moorish slave, Estebanico, entered the region from the south. Their goal was to discover the fabled Seven Cities of Cíbola, which rumor and legend had led the Spanish conquistadors of Mexico to believe was in the north country. Fray Marcos' report to the viceroy of New Spain in September 1539 in turn triggered the famous expedition of the following year, that commanded by Francisco Vásquez de Coronado, who likewise would traverse the San Pedro Valley going north and east in search of riches—little realizing that within just a few miles of his route of march would be discovered one of the world's best-known silver lodes some three and a half centuries later.

The failure of the Coronado expedition meant that once again the land would be controlled solely by its native inhabitants. The enduring and enticing legend of fabulously wealthy cities somewhere to the north would linger and periodically would bring conquistadors and their sons and their grandsons back through the region, but search as they might they never found gold or silver in the San Pedro Valley. They were concentrating their efforts to the north and east. In fact, the first European settlements within a hundred leagues of that area came about not for hope of material gain but rather for hope of a spiritual reward. In the last years of the seventeenth and first years of the eighteenth century, a remarkable Jesuit missionary, Eusebio Francisco Kino, sought to convert the Pimas, Papagos, and Sobaipuris, and to that end constructed rude preaching stations, known as *visitas*, at Tumacácori, Guevavi, and San Xavier del Bac—all three in the next watershed to the west, the Santa Cruz River Valley. Following Kino's death in 1711, itinerant Jesuits visited this region periodically to preach their Christian message, but not until 1732 was a permanent missionary stationed at Guevavi.

The Sobaipuris and Pimas were little inclined to submit to the restricting confines of the mission, however, whereas the warlike Apaches would raid the religious establishments with wearisome regularity. Thus the missionaries began petitioning for military protection, which led in 1742 to the founding of a *presidio* (fort) garrisoned by fifty soldiers at San Phelipe de Guevavi; this was located at the site of an Indian village known as San Mateo de Terrenate in present-day Sonora (just to the south of the Huachuca Mountains), and thus was known familiarly as Terrenate. Thirty-three years later, in 1775, the presidio of Terrenate was moved seven miles southeast to an arroyo known as Las Nutrias, but late that year Spanish officials decided that it should be removed northward to contend with the ever-present Apache menace. The fifty troops traveled north to build new walls and new homes at a site known as Quiburi (near the present town of Fairbanks). Civilian settlers came to farm in the shadow of this fortress, while the soldiers brought their families; together these formed the nucleus of a civil settlement. But Santa Cruz de Terrenate, as the presidio was known, proved to be located astride an Apache war trail, one which brought such violent attacks that in the late 1770s the site was ordered abandoned. A few soldiers did remain at the San Pedro site, and thereby near a large body of rich silver ore, until as late as 1788.[1]

Far more Spaniards lived in the next valley westward, the Santa Cruz, establishing a presidio at Tubac in 1753, which was moved north to Tucson late in 1776. And the missions of Tumacácori and San Xavier del Bac remained viable religious establishments until the end of the Spanish period, although Guevavi was abandoned after 1767. There were approximately six hundred Spaniards in the region. Even though they carried with them samples of gold and silver ore and showed them to the natives with promises of riches if they found duplicates of the ore anywhere, no discoveries were made in the San Pedro Valley. Similarly, the few ranchers, who ventured into the San Pedro region when peace was secured with the Apaches following 1787, found nothing on their land grants; three of these were made, the San Rafael del Valle and the San Juan de las Boquillas y Nogales along the San Pedro, and the San Ignacio del Babocomari between the Huachuca and Whetstone mountains.

Nor did the situation change with the end of Spanish control in 1821 and the emergence of the Republic of Mexico. The last mission in Arizona closed in 1828, but the presidio at Tucson remained exactly the same—with the exception of the flag flying overhead. Arizona in 1846 was still largely the domain of Indians, some six hundred Christian Mexicans holding a precarious bit of land in the vicinity of Tucson and southward up the Santa Cruz Valley toward Sonora.

Then in 1846 came Americans, soldiers commanded by General Stephen Watts Kearny. His "Army of the West," numbering some one hundred dragoons, marched down the Gila River to California, while Lieutenant Colonel Philip St. George Cooke's Mormon Battalion traveled westward along the present Arizona-Sonora boundary to the Santa Cruz Valley, thence to Tucson, which it captured, and on to the Gila and to San Diego, California. At the end of the war between the United States and Mexico in 1848, the Treaty

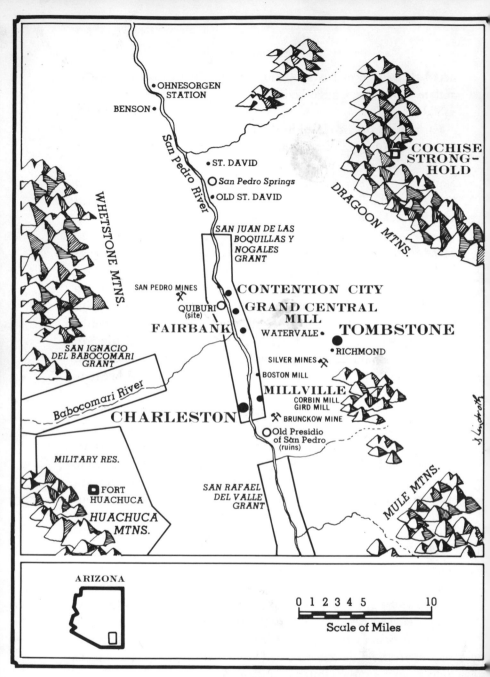

MAP 1 San Pedro Valley

of Guadalupe Hidalgo was signed and Arizona north of the Gila River was transferred to the United States. Then almost six years later the Gadsden Purchase agreement established the present boundary between the two republics. The San Pedro Valley—and its unsuspected silver ore—had become American property.

The year 1849 saw widespread entry of Americans into Arizona, but as transients, not residents. These were the Forty-niners using the wagon road pioneered by Cooke and the Mormon Battalion. Dubbed the Gila Trail, this route was chosen by some nine thousand hopefuls in that one year alone, and by some sixty thousand in the three-year period 1849-51. Those who stayed in the region, which was part of the Territory of New Mexico in 1850, were small in number. A few permanent residents chose to farm, some became ranchers, and a score or so opened stores; but primarily it was Arizona's mineral wealth—or the search for it—that later lured men to what seemed to them a harsh country. Desert heat and aridity, along with fierce Indian warriors, induced little settlement, but gold and silver overcame reluctance to fight obstacles. Coming to Arizona first to quest for precious metals was Charles DeBrille Poston, who also brought to Arizona the first miner in the San Pedro Valley.

A native of Kentucky, Poston in 1850, at the age of twenty-five, moved to San Francisco, where he became chief clerk in the surveyor's office at the customs house. When news of the impending Gadsden Purchase reached that city late in 1853, Poston became very excited and was easily persuaded by a French syndicate to lead an expedition to southern Arizona in search of silver. Recruiting twenty-five men, Poston sailed for Guaymas, Sonora, in February 1854 aboard a British ship, the *Zoraida*. Unfortunately this vessel was wrecked in the Gulf of California on the coast of the Mexican state of Sinaloa, but he and all his men reached shore safely. Then they marched northward, up through Sinaloa and Sonora into southern Arizona. South of Tucson in the Santa Cruz Valley they found a strong indication of silver deposits and of abandoned Spanish mines.

Satisfied there was rich ore there, Poston led his men north to Tucson and the Gila River, which they followed to Fort Yuma. There he met Major Samuel P. Heintzelman, commanding officer of the post, and they excitedly discussed the possibilities. Poston then continued to California to report to the French syndicate—after which he journeyed to Cincinnati, Ohio, Heintzelman's home town, where the Sonora Exploring and Mining Company was capitalized at $1,000,000, $100,000 paid in. The new firm listed Heintzelman as president; Poston, as general manager, had orders to hire employees and to establish mines in Arizona. He recruited employees in San Antonio, Texas, men he later described as "armed with Sharp's rifles, Colt's revolvers, and the recklessness of youth."

One of those reckless young men hired by Poston was Frederick Brunckow, who astonishingly was a graduate of the School of Mines at Freiburg in Saxony, Germany. Born of a Russian father and German mother in 1820 in Berlin (then the capital of Prussia), Brunckow had received a classical education at the University of Westphalia and then at Freiburg, at that time probably the best school in the world in geology and mining engineering. He became involved in the revolutionary upheavals in Germany in 1848, as did many university students, and had to flee after their failure. He arrived in the United States at New York in 1850. Then he got a job as a deck hand on a steamboat and worked his way down the Mississippi. Eventually he arrived at New Braunfels, Texas, a German community where doubtless he did not feel so foreign. There Poston found him working as a shingle-maker for $2.50 a week plus board. Brunckow enthusiastically signed on as an employee of the Sonora Exploring and Mining Company, a position for which his education and inclination had eminently prepared him.

Poston led his employees westward from San Antonio, celebrating the Fourth of July at El Paso and arriving in Tucson in August. The abandoned Spanish presidio at Tubac became headquarters for the company, for the buildings were still standing. The commanding officer's quarters became the company headquarters, while the barracks became rooms for the men. The old guardhouse afforded ample storeroom for company property, and the presidial tower, three stories of which were still intact, was ideal for posting sentries to watch for marauding Apaches. Poston sent men to the Santa Rita Mountains to cut timber for doors and windows, and within a short time Tubac again was in good physical condition. Next he and the men explored the countryside, and soon several mines were opened, the best of which was named the Heintzelman. This mine had been worked slightly in Spanish-Mexican days, when it was known as the Cerro Colorado; under Poston's supervision it was made to produce handsomely. In 1859 this company bought a European barrel-amalgamating works in San Francisco for $30,000; this was transported by ship to Yuma, then brought overland to Tubac where it was erected near the Heintzelman Mine, and soon approximately $3000 a day in silver was coming from it.

Supplies to feed the miners and other employees of the company were easily obtained. Wild game—quail, ducks, and deer—abounded in the vicinity, so that even a poor hunter could keep the dining table well supplied with meat. Poston hired a German gardener who fenced in and cultivated a field with irrigation water from the Santa Cruz River, thereby providing fresh vegetables. And at the abandoned mission in nearby Tumacácori, the orchards planted by the long-dead padres still were bearing fruit. In addition, beef, flour, beans, sugar, and coffee could be obtained from Sonora at reasonable prices. Thus the company's table, open free of charge to travelers, became famous for the richness and diversity of its spread.

Poston even had his men dig deep pools beside the Santa Cruz River; shaded by trees, they were cool bathing places. According to witnesses, Poston "used to sit in the water, like the Englishman in Hyperion, and read the newspapers, by which means he kept his temper cool amid the various disturbing influences which surrounded him." Of this period at Tubac, when Arizona was yet a part of New Mexico Territory and civil officials of all types were virtually unknown, Poston later reminisced, "We had no law but love, and no occupation but labor. No government, no taxes, no public debt, no politics. It was a community in a perfect state of nature."

But in this paradise there was a snake. Most of the common laborers were Mexicans from nearby Sonora, then as now going north of the border for higher wages and better opportunities. The police on both sides of the border was not effective and when a constant vigil was not kept, the laborers were able to murder their gringo employers, steal the silver and supplies, and flee southward. Also there was the ever-constant threat of Apache attacks.

In this difficult and dangerous situation in southern Arizona, Frederick Brunckow rose rapidly in the Sonora Exploring and Mining Company so that by 1859 his annual salary was $1800. His knowledge of mining engineering was of great value to Poston, especially Brunckow's ability with the blow-pipe and his willingness to instruct the other German employees in the proper grading of ore. Moreover, Brunckow had an excellent social background, was a keen sportsman, was fond of the chase, and, according to Poston, "added to his accomplishments the pleasing quality of being an excellent dresser of wild game."

In 1858 Poston found it expedient to send Brunckow, along with several other engineers and employees, to New York to give information about the mines of Arizona to company stockholders and financiers. Thus, later wrote Poston, Brunckow and the others "were enabled to transfer the festivities of Tubac to Delmonicos [restaurant], where the pioneers unfolded to the capitalists of Gotham the wonders of the Arizona mines."

Apparently this trip either convinced Brunckow to form his own mining concern, or else he found the capital he needed to finance a previously made decision to strike out on his own. As early as February 1857 he had filed a claim in his own name, one located in the San Pedro Valley—which therefore he had prospected. Thus in 1859, upon his return to Arizona, he resigned his position with the Sonora Exploring and Mining Company, moved to the San

Pedro Valley, and established a mining concern known as the St. Louis Mining Company. His mine, located near the bank of the San Pedro River near the site where Charleston and Millville later would be located, was called the Brunckow, but this often was corrupted into "Broncho."[2] Apparently his venture was successful, for the census of 1860 listed him as residing at the "San Pedro Silver Mines," age forty, with property valued at $12,000.[3]

In this risky venture, Brunckow had two partners, brothers named James and William M. Williams. These two men, natives of Virginia and Pennsylvania and thirty-three and twenty-five years old, respectively, had lived in St. Louis, and both had background knowledge of engineering. Joining them in the effort as an employee was J. C. Moss, formerly a teacher of chemistry in a high school in St. Louis and a native Pennsylvanian. At the Brunckow Mine they exposed a vein apparently rich in silver, and there they erected buildings and a store. To do the actual labor in the mines, they imported laborers from Sonora, as was the usual practice; David Brontrager, a German employed to cook for all of them, later declared that eleven Mexicans had been hired and that they had brought with them three or four women and two or three children. This constituted a sizable community for an area so exposed to Apache attack.

Brunckow and his partners apparently became careless about their Mexican employees, for on July 23, 1860, came disaster. While William M. Williams was absent to get supplies at Fort Buchanan, an army post established in 1856 some fifty miles to the northwest, the laborers decided to kill their employers. Brontrager, the cook, later stated that he was in the kitchen sitting by the stove and reading a book when two Mexicans came in, asking if they could light their cigars from the cookstove. Suddenly he heard shots. But when he arose to see what had happened, the two Mexicans told him to remain where he was. In a few moments the other peons came in to inform him that all the others were dead; naturally he feared for his life, but he was told he would be spared because he was a Catholic. Then methodically the Mexicans packed everything of value: $2000 worth of goods recently brought from St. Louis, a steam engine not yet fully assembled, some money, and what little jewelry they could find, along with four animals. All this they took with them. They also took the terrified cook, whom they released only after having traveled thirty miles toward Mexico.

William M. Williams meanwhile returned from his errand at Fort Buchanan. He arrived after dark and was surprised to find the buildings unlighted. Entering one of them, he stumbled over a body while searching for matches. Stooping to see what he had tripped on, he groped and his hand touched a pool of blood. Still in the dark, he made his way into another room, only to fall over yet another body. Still not having found matches with which to light a lamp, he ran out, mounted his horse, and galloped back to the fort, all the while not knowing if his brother was alive or dead. He reached Buchanan at daybreak, and a detachment of soldiers quickly was readied to return to the mine with him. They discovered that the two bodies in the building were his brother James and J. C. Moss. Brunckow's corpse was found only after a long search; it was at the bottom of a mining shaft half a mile away, a rock drill jammed through the body. The three men were buried there without markers for their graves.

When the cook, Brontrager, finally stumbled into the fort after being freed by his abductors, he was half incoherent with fear, and for a time he was held as a possible perpetrator of the crime. But gradually his story was checked. Mexican authorities were informed of what he claimed had transpired, and they told the Americans that the story was true. Some of the goods taken by the Mexican miners were recovered, but not one of the miners was ever captured and returned to Arizona for trial.[4]

It was shortly after the first effort at mining in the San Pedro Valley ended in tragic failure that the Civil War began and all American soldiers in southern Arizona were withdrawn to protect New Mexico from Confederate invasion. This occurred just as the Chiricahua Apaches, led by Cochise, thundered out of a period of relative peace to attack the remaining Americans as a result of the

Bascom Affair. Started by a drunken rancher, John Ward, who falsely accused Cochise and his Apache followers of kidnapping his stepson, the incident was climaxed by an abortive attempt to arrest Cochise by Lieutenant George N. Bascom at Apache Pass. Thereafter the Chiricahua leader took delight in revenging himself on those Americans he could find in southern Arizona, principally miners and ranchers.

In addition to the Apache menace, there were Mexican outlaws operating in the region. Because of the unsettled political conditions in that republic during the Civil War years and immediately afterward, there was no effective police system in Sonora. Banditry and smuggling were rampant. Mining activity virtually ceased in southern Arizona. The census of 1864, taken the year after Arizona was given separate territorial status, listed only three men as residing at "San Pedro." All were native New Mexicans: Miguel Alejo, age thirty-one; Stanislado Gándara, age thirty-two; and Miguel Torres, age thirty-two. All described themselves as single, and all gave their occupation as laborer. Possibly there were others living in the region, however, for a note appended to this census location stated, "Incomplete will send in supplement. . . . (No supplement was found)."[5] This census does indicate that a small amount of mining was continuing in the San Pedro Valley, probably at the Brunckow Mine, despite the hazards of the age.

The next owner of record of the Brunckow was the man responsible for taking the census of 1864, at the time a United States marshal, Milton B. Duffield. Fifty-four years of age, this native of Virginia came to Arizona in 1864 after a career that saw him at one time involved in mercantile pursuits, a Forty-niner, a real estate trader in California, and an Indian fighter. Known as "the Major," he was reputed a legendary shot when he came to the territory, but he also came under a cloud of suspicion of fraud in his previous place of residence, California. Once in Arizona, he established a reputation for ferocity, bravery, and a willingness to shoot quickly. And he was a walking arsenal. On one occasion in a bar, he was asked to show all the weapons of violence he had on his body; he

Milton B. Duffield, the United States Marshal for Arizona Territory who at one time owned the Brunckow Mine. *Courtesy Arizona Historical Society.*

proceeded to lay on the bar no fewer than twelve items: guns, knives, and assorted other hardware of a deadly kind.

He resigned his badge as a United States marshal when he grew tired of the scant salary he was receiving, but he did not leave Arizona. Instead he settled in the southern part of the territory where, according to his biographer, he was known in his old age as "fearless, domineering, hard-drinking, the perennial champion of his own opinions and the harsh critic of his fellow officers. . . ."[6] In 1871, for example, he was brought to trial for assaulting the editor of the Tucson *Weekly Citizen*, but in court drew his pistol and walked out, a free man whom no one dared arrest again. Tempestuous and quarrelsome, the Major never hesitated to involve himself in quarrels—or even to write President Ulysses S. Grant about his difficulties and to inform him, the President, that his, Duffield's, adversaries were scoundrels.

And in 1873 he had more than enough to complain about. On August 7 that year in the Old Pueblo (Tucson), Vicente Hernandez, a local merchant, and his wife were brutally murdered. A vigilante group quickly formed, the guilty parties were apprehended the next day, and a public gathering roared the sentence for those captured, "Death!" A fourth murderer was convicted by the courts and was awaiting an appeal to a higher court when preparations were made to hang all four of them. Only one man in Tucson protested—Milton B. Duffield, for the fourth man to be hanged was named John Willis and, said Duffield to the crowd, "You can hang a Mexican . . . but you can't hang an American citizen!" He shouted this in a voice whose volume was aided by alcohol, but the crowd was not in a mood to tolerate interruptions. Duffield was overpowered, taken to the courthouse, and jailed while the hangings proceeded. Later, when Duffield was released, he decided to seek revenge for the indignities heaped on him by clubbing William Zechendorf, a merchant who had led the vigilantes. Yet even here Duffield was to be disappointed, for Zechendorf proved a more formidable opponent than the Major had anticipated; he hit Duffield, knocked him to the ground, and then administered a sound thrashing. That evening, in his cups, the Major became embroiled in yet another fight, this one with yet another man, and again he was a loser. He ended that sad and doubtless memorable day by fighting a Mexican—who administered him yet a third beating.

The Brunckow Mine probably seemed a less formidable opponent for Duffield than the residents of Tucson. He had claimed the mine as early as 1864, but the records of Pima County reveal that he formally purchased it from Mervin G. Gay and others on October 23, 1866.[7] How Mervin Gay acquired title to sell is unknown. But unquestioned ownership of the Brunckow brought Duffield yet another quarrel, this one fatal, for there was a rival claimant to ownership. In fact, Joseph T. Holmes in asserting his title to the mine decided to move into the abandoned buildings. Duffield on June 5, 1874, decided to evict his rival. In company with Joseph Oligher, he rode to the Brunckow and forced an entrance into the building Holmes was occupying. Holmes, who knew that Duffield had threatened to kill everyone at the Brunckow, grabbed a double-barreled gun and told the Major to advance no farther. Duffield was never one to allow himself to be ordered about; he kept coming, whereupon Holmes emptied both barrels into him. The Major died shortly afterward of a gunshot wound in the head. Holmes was brought to trial for the killing, convicted of voluntary manslaughter, and sentenced to three years' imprisonment. After serving only seventeen days, however, he escaped and was never recaptured. Duffield's body was buried on the San Pedro near Frederick Brunckow and the others who had been murdered by Mexican employees fourteen years previously.

Less than a month after the Major was shot, Mrs. Mary E. Vaughn placed an advertisement in the Tucson *Citizen* of July 4, 1874, to warn against trespassing at the Brunckow Mine. She claimed to have bought the mine from Duffield more than a year previously, and her assertion, when checked, was substantiated by the Pima County Book of Mines. Apparently the Major, who was in financial difficulty during his last few years of life, had transferred the title to Mrs. Vaughn, his "housekeeper" from 1871 to 1874, to prevent the mine from being taken by his creditors.[8]

Sidney R. DeLong, part-owner of the Brunckow Mine in 1877 when
Ed Schieffelin was hired as a guard there. *Courtesy Arizona Historical
Society*.

Mrs. Vaughn was unable to retain ownership of the Brunckow, however. Three years later, Sydney R. DeLong had become the principal owner, along with two partners, Tom Jeffords and a man known as Rodgers. DeLong, a member of the Council in the 8th Territorial Legislature, was born in New York in 1828, had moved to California in 1849, had joined the First California Infantry during the Civil War, and had moved to Arizona after the war. Settling in Tucson, he worked for the freighting firm of Tully & Ochoa until 1867, when he purchased and became editor of the *Southern Arizonian*, a newspaper whose name he changed in 1868 to the *Weekly Arizonian*. By training DeLong was an engineer and surveyor, but as an editor he prospered because Tucson at the time was the capital of the territory and he was astute enough to sell an interest in the paper to Governor Richard C. McCormick. In January 1869 DeLong divested himself of his interest in the newspaper. He became post trader at Fort Bowie, an army post established at Apache Pass in 1862, and simultaneously he was postmaster for the camp. The location at which he worked gave him proximity to the San Pedro Valley, while the positions he occupied allowed him time to investigate the mineral potential of the Brunckow Mine. Thus he was interested in them. And in 1872, when he returned to Tucson and was elected its mayor, he began working quietly to acquire title to the abandoned mine.

Tom Jeffords, a minor partner in this venture, is best remembered as the white friend of the Chiricahua chieftain, Cochise, with whom he possibly was a "blood brother." Of Rodgers, little is known except that he was murdered by the Apaches, apparently in 1876. His body was buried near those of Brunckow and Duffield.[9]

Thus in 1877 the only evidence of mining in the San Pedro Valley was the crumbling buildings which Brunckow had erected, along with the graves—possibly even the ghosts—of three consecutive owners of the claim. Yet those shacks and graves were the stuff of legends, for around them would be built rumors of rich silver deposits awaiting intrepid, enterprising men who through boldness and bravery might ferret out the wealth of the San Pedro Valley.

A few men did remember that Brunckow frequently had stated that in the valley "would be discovered someday vast mineral treasures."[10] The Mine he had opened was still there, and DeLong and Jeffords were yet performing the necessary annual assessment work to retain their title. But as the year 1877 began, no real mining was taking place in the region. The silver that was beneath the ground was awaiting a discoverer.

The Discovery

In the spring of 1877 Arizona's economic growth was at low ebb. The first flurry of mining, which had brought separate territorial status in 1863, had passed. The Walker Mining District in the vicinity of Prescott had ceased to yield more than meager returns, although an occasional new discovery would cause a brief stir of excitement and optimistic talk. Even the great Silver King Mine and the town of Pinal in east-central Arizona were declining. One or two mines in the northern part of the territory were producing, but not in sufficient quantity to cause a boom. At Clifton, meanwhile, a few entrepreneurs were struggling valiantly in an effort to open the copper bodies to commercial development; and copper had been discovered at Globe, but as of 1877 was not being worked much. Almost all the silver mines to the south and southeast of Tucson had been closed. Nor was ranching producing handsome returns because of the difficulty of getting cattle to market; only the reservations and the army posts offered the possibility of sales. The railroad had not yet arrived, although the Southern Pacific's tracks were inching slowly eastward from San Diego toward Yuma Crossing, while the Texas and Pacific was hardly beyond Fort Worth as it built westward.

Compounding the problem of developing the economic potential of Arizona at this time were the Indian disturbances, especially in the southeastern part of the territory. Following the tragic Bascom Affair, the Chiricahua Apaches made life and property extremely unsafe in this area, even after the return of troops following the end of the Civil War. Finally in 1871 a federal peace commission came to Arizona; headed by Vincent Colyer, a mild-mannered Quaker, it was able to persuade some four thousand Indians to accept reservations. When Colyer departed, the only major tribe of Apaches not on reservations was the Chiricahuas, still led by Cochise. And that was remedied in 1872 when Brigadier General Oliver Otis Howard, a one-armed veteran of the Civil War known to his troops as "Bible-Quoting Howard," came to Arizona as head of yet another peace commission. He inspected the military posts in the Department of Arizona, arranged conferences with the Pimas, Papagos, and other tribes, and moved one agency northward to the Gila River where it was renamed San Carlos. Thereafter San Carlos was to be the major reservation for Apaches. Finally, with the assistance of Thomas J. Jeffords, Howard met the aging Cochise in a dramatic confrontation; arriving unarmed and accompanied only by Jeffords, Howard persuaded the Chiricahua chieftain to accept a peace treaty. By this the Chiricahuas were given a reservation approximately fifty-five miles square in southeastern Arizona, including the Dragoon and Chiricahua mountains and the Sulphur Springs and San Simon valleys, the traditional homeland of the tribe—and with Tom Jeffords as their agent.

Until the death of Cochise in 1874, the Chiricahuas honored this agreement despite the pleas of their eastern cousins, the Warm Springs Apaches, who wanted them to go on the warpath. Cochise was succeeded as chief by his son Taza, and there followed two years of hardship, unrest, and disaster, culminating on May 3, 1876, when Apache Indian Agent John P. Clum received orders from Washington to close the Chiricahua reservation and to move this tribe to San Carlos. Clum arrived at the old agency on June 6 and six days later began to move north accompanied by Taza and 325 Chiricahuas; however, more than 400 of the tribesmen refused to make the move and fled to Mexico under the leadership of Juh, Nolgee, and a rising war leader named Geronimo. The removal of the Chiricahuas to San Carlos proved a disastrous mistake. The various bands of Apaches at San Carlos hated each other, and most of them were homesick for their traditional homelands. Shorted on their promised rations, and forced to farm, they became angry and resentful, willing recruits for any warrior who promised them loot and adventure off the reservation. During the next five years, until they made a major break from San Carlos, these unhappy people made life and property unsafe in southern Arizona and northern Sonora.[1]

What Arizona most needed in the spring of 1877 was some economic shot which would bring both money and people to its arid reaches. And, as usually happens, the discovery arrived with muffled oars. The opening of the rich silver lodes of the San Pedro Valley came about inadvertently.

That spring Sydney R. DeLong and his partners, owners of the Brunckow Mine, had to perform their annual assessment work in order to retain ownership of it. According to federal mining laws, anyone with a mining claim on public lands had to perform one hundred dollars' worth of work on it during the first ninety days to validate the claim, and thereafter one hundred dollars' worth of work on it annually. This was called assessment work. But securing men to do assessment work on the Brunckow was not easy that spring of 1877 despite the recent erection of Fort Huachuca some thirty miles to the west. It had been established on March 3, 1877, on the northeast side of the Huachuca Mountains by troops of the 6th Cavalry to prevent renegade Apaches from raiding into Mexico. At first it was considered a temporary encampment, but on January 21, 1878, it was made a permanent post.[2] DeLong and his partners could promise military protection to their employees, but most residents of southern Arizona knew that the Apaches were lifting the hair of straggling prospectors and unwary cowboys.

However, they finally were able to hire two men to do this assessment work at the Brunckow. These two men departed Tucson and slipped southeastward. On their way toward their destination in the San Pedro Valley, they stopped at the camp of George Woolfolk, who had just arrived a few days previously to attempt ranching in the area. At Woolfolk's camp, the two miners met a young man of large and powerful build, one standing just half an inch under six feet tall and weighing some 175 pounds. He had a good outfit, an excellent rifle, and plenty of ammunition. On the spot they hired him out of their own pockets to stand guard while they did the necessary assessment work at the Brunckow Mine. Thus was Edward Lawrence Schieffelin brought to his rendezvous with riches.

The discoverer of the silver mines of the San Pedro Valley in Arizona epitomized the hopes and dreams of every sourdough prospector who ever wandered the lonely mountains, valleys, and streams of the American West. By 1877 he already had searched in vain for years and had lived at the edge of starvation, secretly nourishing all the while his hope of discovering a bonanza. Ed Schieffelin was born in Tioga County, Pennsylvania, in October 1847. In company with his father, Clinton Schieffelin, he westered to the Rogue River country of Oregon in the late 1850s to pan for gold, thereby beginning his lifelong career as a prospector. Once experienced, the life was so enticing that no other mode of existence was thinkable; the true prospector was imbued with a feverish restlessness that made the benefits of a more civilized place of residence and steady employment not worth the freedom that he believed he lost in the process.

For the prospector, as for the mountain man who had preceded him, the settled and secure life was boring beyond toleration. He took a washing pan and a grubstake, and with boundless optimism he climbed the mountains and tramped the deserts. He panned each promising stream, often standing for hours waist deep in icy waters, and he broke pieces from every outcropping of rock, always looking for that telltale glint of precious metal. When he ran out of food and was unable to subsist on the game he brought down with his rifle, he tried to interest some merchant in advancing him credit for an outfit in return for a share in the lode he knew he shortly would find. And, as a last resort, he would take a job, painfully saving the necessary few dollars with which to grubstake himself for yet another go at finding his pot of gold. Even when he did discover this, as happened to a few of them, he usually did not try to develop the mine himself; rather he would sell it as quickly as possible to some mining syndicate and use the money for a prolonged spree, enriching bartenders and the girls at some "hog ranch" until he was broke again. Then he set out to search for yet another lode.

Ed Schieffelin was of this breed—to a point. He was that rarest of Westerners, a teetotaler, neither drinking nor gambling nor yet indulging himself in spending sprees. In point of truth, he could not have done these things even had he been so inclined, for Ed Schieffelin had no luck during his first twenty-nine years. He had wandered from Oregon through Idaho, Nevada, Utah, and California without success, accepting periodic employment to finance his prospecting ventures. In 1873 he was at Eureka, California, where for eighteen months he tried the regular life, working at various employments. But after a year and a half, he decided that he was "no better off than I was prospecting, and not half so well satisfied." Thus he decided to return to that existence, but first he needed money.

From Eureka he journeyed to Austin where he joined his brother, Albert E. Schieffelin, in chopping wood by the cord during the winter of 1874-75. Later he recalled that he intended to save sufficient funds to finance a prospecting venture in Arizona, an area he previously had not visited. Just as he had accumulated the funds, however, he became ill with what he diagnosed as mountain fever; not wanting to go to a physician, for he and most people at the time rightfully distrusted medical practitioners, he began traveling in search of a healthier climate. By the fall of 1875 he was on the stage road from Winnemucca, Nevada, to Silver City, Idaho, leading horses for a stage company, his health no better than when he had departed Austin. And, as always, he was short of money.

Ed Schieffelin, discoverer of Tombstone. *Courtesy Arizona Historical Society.*

Sick men often begin to long for home, and that to him was Oregon. He had decided "that wet country would cure me, if anything would. . . ." In November 1875 he set out, traveling by stagecoach. On the way from Redding, California, to his parents' home, the stage was caught in a severe storm which "left me entirely cured of the fever, but with a bad cough." Twenty-eight years old, the six-year-absent prodigal arrived at his destination with only $2.50 in his pocket. And he was discouraged to note that wages in Oregon were high and that men who had remained at home, men he had known previously, had become prosperous while he was off prospecting. Perhaps it was a feeling that fortune had passed him by which prompted him in less than three weeks to borrow $100 from his father and to depart Oregon for Arizona.

Again it was by stagecoach south to Redding, from whence he took the newly built railroad to Colston, finally to arrive at San Bernardino. Again traveling by stage, he pushed eastward toward Arizona, but his money gave out at Ivanpah. He arrived there with $1.25 in his pocket, his blankets on his back—and his dinner that evening cost a dollar. For the next fourteen months he worked at a steady job, living as frugally as possible in order to save enough money to buy a prospecting outfit. Finally in January 1877 he was able to get exactly what he wanted: two good mules, saddles, arms, ammunition, and food. He was a determined man when he turned his back on Ivanpah: "I had a good outfit, and made up my mind, no matter what occurred, I would keep it, and if I could not do any better I would live off my rifle until I found a prospect." Nor was he especially concerned about the menace of the Indians; later he recalled, "I wasn't looking for bullets but I felt if one happened my way it wouldn't make much difference to anyone but me, and I never could figure out that to be dead would be unpleasant. Some people seem to know all about such things but I'm a bit stupid I suppose for I've never been able to learn the alphabet of birth and death."

His initial idea was to search in the vicinity of the Grand Canyon, but a two-month look at the undisturbed sedimentary strata on top and the barren schists below convinced him there was no mining future there. While he was at the Grand Canyon, however, he learned that a group of Hualapai Indians were being enlisted to go to southern Arizona to scout against the Apache renegades. He thought he would follow along with them, thereby gaining protection from hostile Indians as he prospected. Thus in company with this party he arrived at Fort Huachuca about April 1, 1877. For the next few days he used the fort as a base of supply, going out each day to prospect and returning to it at night for protection. And when a detail of troops took the field for a few days, he would travel with them. However, he quickly decided that following the soldiers did not allow him really to prospect, for they were following Indians and not riding up canyons that showed mineral promise. Therefore he determined to strike out on his own; he would still use Fort Huachuca as his supply base, returning there periodically to get what he needed. But for protection against the Apaches he would use his own eyes and his rifle. The soldiers at the fort did not think this sufficient, nor did they believe he would find gold or silver. Thus when he did come in to re-supply, they would ask him derisively if he had found anything. When he replied that he as yet had made no discovery, they would tell him that all he would find out there was his "tombstone."

It was not long after this that he stopped at George Woolfolk's ranch and there was hired by the two men doing assessment work at the Brunckow Mine. The employment he accepted because it meant hard cash which he could use to buy yet more supplies and continue his prospect. But even while standing guard at the Brunckow, Schieffelin used the time to good advantage. With field glasses he surveyed the region, especially the Tombstone hills with their weathered, bleached, gray-granite faults running southeast and northwest. He spent hours looking at the faults and synclines, for he knew these to be an indication of a geologic upheaval—and thus potentially rich in minerals.

The assessment work done, Schieffelin took his pay and set out on a trip to this area, and there he found promising "float" (chunks of ore which had broken off from a major lode and which had been carried down into the valley by water—hence the name float). That night he returned to camp with the two workers, who had not yet departed; they had decided to go to Tucson to get their pay and then to return to the San Pedro Valley to ranch some thirty miles to the north (near the present Benson). To one of them, William Griffith, the float looked sufficiently promising that he made Schieffelin an offer: he would furnish provisions, supply the cash to have assays made, and pay for recording the claims; in turn, Schieffelin would locate not one but two claims adjoining one another, one for himself and one for Griffith. To this Schieffelin agreed, further stipulating that afterward one of them would build the monument of location and the other would have his choice of the two claims. But there were to be no additional partners. They sealed this agreement with a handshake, and the two would-be ranchers departed for Tucson.

When the two men returned, however, Griffith had changed his mind. In Tucson he had talked with a man named Lee, the owner of a flour mill, who had advised him to settle 640 acres in the San Pedro Valley under the terms of the Desert Land Act[3] and that he, Lee, would then furnish the funds to prepare it for irrigation. This, Griffith had decided, was a more certain way to wealth than prospecting, for Lee had agreed to purchase all the grain he grew. Therefore he terminated his agreement with Schieffelin—who meanwhile had located the stipulated two claims. One of these he had named the Tombstone, and the other later would be called the Graveyard. Schieffelin even took Griffith to the spot and showed the two claims to him, but Griffith remained adamant; he said he could not both farm and mine—and he preferred the former. Thus he departed downriver to locate his 640 acres, leaving Schieffelin to continue his prospecting.

He was not alone, however. The valley of the San Pedro was considered prime country for ranching except for the danger of Indian raids. Despite this menace, there were a number of hardy pioneers willing to risk their hair and their lives in order to locate good grass, and thus Schieffelin had company with which to huddle together at night for protection. Among those ranchers who came to stay or to camp there temporarily were George Woolfolk, Albert Smith, two brothers named Bullard, and two other men called Landers and Sampson. Even a small party of people calling themselves the Chicago Colony, bound for a spot below Tres Alamos (a stage station better known as Dunbar's Station located on the San Pedro River thirty-five miles east of Tucson) stopped for a few days. Schieffelin would leave this camp early in the morning to trek into the Tombstone country, remain overnight, and then return to the general camp the following evening.

In this manner he had a good look at the country, which proved difficult to prospect. Later it would be ascertained that the mining district which Schieffelin was investigating—and would discover—extended about eight miles east and west and about five miles north and south. This was situated in a series of rolling hills which gradually ascended until they merged into the Mule Mountains on the south, and which stretched away in an undulating plain to the Dragoon range on the north. The geological formation of the district presented several unusual features: porphyry was the predominant rock but with an overlay of lime above the ore bodies. And quartzite was everywhere, although a granite formation was on the western edge of the district. However, once shafts were sunk and depth was attained, the surface lime ended, with porphyry and quartzite constituting most of what then was found.[4]

Schieffelin later would comment about his search that it "was pretty slow work . . . until you once learned the country, then it went fast enough." Still he did not find any of the principal mines that summer of 1877, the ones that later would yield such spectacular results. Rather he picked up bits and pieces of float and chunks of ore, enough to satisfy himself that rich mines eventually would be located in the area. His major worry as he worked was the Indian menace. Renegade Chiricahuas were known to be lurking in the area, making life unsafe not only for the lone prospector or rancher but even for parties of considerable size. And Cochise's

Stronghold, a favorite site of the Chiricahuas in the Dragoons, was across the relatively flat valley to the northwest, and in the clear air the slightest dust he raised could be seen for miles.

About August 1, his brief former partner Griffith relayed word to Schieffelin, by a man bound upriver toward Mexico, to come north, bringing with him ore samples and copies of location notices for the two mines that had been found so that they could go together to Tucson and have them recorded. He apparently had changed his mind. And the two of them did go to the Old Pueblo, arriving there during the feast of San Juan during the last week of August. Unfortunately no assayer was in Tucson to test the ores and pieces of float and thus to render an accurate verdict as to their worth. Thus Griffith, who knew many of the local residents, took the samples and showed them to his acquaintances, hoping thereby to gain a backer. Included were ore samples from the claim Schieffelin had labeled the Graveyard, a ledge that later would prove to be of little value. Little wonder then that Griffith's friends did not have much interest in the samples. In fact, those who bothered to look—and almost every man in the region considered himself an expert on ores—pronounced them out-of-hand to be of little value. Again Griffith became discouraged, and only at Schieffelin's strong urging did he bother to record the Graveyard in his name and the Tombstone in Schieffelin's name. Ironically it was the other ores in Schieffelin's possession, the ones which did not appear very promising, which later proved to come from the richest mines in the Tombstone District—and these the two men did not record.

One of the men to whom Griffith showed the samples was Sydney R. DeLong, part-owner of the Brunckow Mine. DeLong, without bothering to look at them more than in a cursory way, stated that he had all the mines he wanted and that he was not interested in acquiring ownership of any additional ones. Griffith had not made him an offer, but apparently DeLong concluded that such was his intent.

And Schieffelin encountered the same attitude wherever he went. When he walked into Tully & Ochoa's store to purchase supplies with his last six dollars, the men there asked him what he was doing. He replied that he was prospecting in the San Pedro Valley, whereupon knowing old-timers asked why he did not become a rancher; the grass there was good, the land was free for the taking, and money could be made. To this Schieffelin responded that he did not want to ranch.

"Well," he was told, "A man is foolish to prospect in that country; it takes money to prospect; you can't come in here and get supplies unless you have money to pay for them."

Schieffelin responded that he had sufficient cash to pay for whatever he bought, which was flour and a few other necessities. Schieffelin later recalled dryly, "If I had located a ranch they would have let me have supplies, but a prospector was to be discouraged from the folly of hunting for mines in that country." Actually there were a few residents of the Old Pueblo interested in grubstaking prospectors, but Schieffelin and Griffith did not meet any of them. A description of him, written by a resident of Tucson about this time, stated, "He was about the queerest specimen of humanity ever seen . . . with black curly hair that hung several inches below his shoulders. His long untrimmed beard was a mass of unkempt knots and mats. His clothing was worn out and covered with patches of deerskins, corduroy, and flannel, and his old slouch hat, too, was so pieced with rabbit skin that very little of the original felt remained. Although only twenty-seven years of age he looked at least forty."[5]

That evening Griffith was sorely discouraged and asked Schieffelin what he intended to do. The reply was that of every prospector of the American West, of men who lived on hope: "I am going back; it does not matter to me what these fellows say; I believe that rock is good, and that one of these days there will be something of importance found there, whether we find it or not." Then, drawing from his years of experience prospecting, he concluded, "I have seen enough to show me that there are mines there, and I am going back; you may do as you please." Griffith did not have the experience—or the unbounded optimism—needed and responded that he was through with mining. He was going back to his ranch.

Schieffelin then went to another store to purchase a sack of Mexican flour, which was cheaper than the American equivalent, and some bacon, leaving himself only enough money to have his mule shod at Fort Lowell, the army post nine miles out of town, such work being only half as costly at the military encampment as in town. Then he departed for the San Pedro country. When he arrived at his old campsite (about where Fairbanks now stands), he found only two would-be ranchers, Sampson and Landers, yet there. The others had departed, leaving their belongings behind. Schieffelin stayed with them several days, going out into the hills to prospect during the day and returning to the camp at night. When the two men completed the work in which they had been engaged, Landers departed for Tucson; Sampson stayed with Schieffelin, for he had decided to prospect. They remained despite their uneasiness over the Indian menace; they were determined to look for placer gold in the mountains to the south.

And they made a sweep southward that lasted some twenty-two days—without success. Then, when they returned to their camp-site, it was to discover that all the ranchers in the vicinity had abandoned the region owing to Apache war parties rumored to be in the region. Two adobe cabins on the San Pedro, built the previous summer by some of the ranchers, were empty, everything having been taken out of them. It was at this point, about October 1, that Sampson likewise decided to leave, and he departed for Fort Huachuca, taking with him all the provisions that were left.

His departure reduced Schieffelin, as he later recalled, "to the last extremity." He had no provisions, his clothing was in shreds, and he possessed only thirty cents in cash. Game was plentiful in the vicinity, and so long as he had ammunition he would not starve; but after subsisting on deer meat for several days, he decided that he temporarily would have to abandon the San Pedro Valley. His first thought was of his brother, Albert, who at last notice had been working to the north at the Silver King Mine. Perhaps, he thought, he could interest Albert in joining him in a partnership to prospect the San Pedro country. With Albert's money, they could have Schieffelin's ores assayed, and with that report, if it was favorable as he believed it would be, they probably could secure a grubstake from some merchant. This notion in mind, Schieffelin went back into the Tombstone hills on one last hunt, taking samples of float, outcropping ore, and rock for the assayer.

These in hand, the lonely prospector turned his back on the region he believed would bring him fortune and started down-river. For fifty miles he followed the San Pedro northward, then struck out cross-country for the Globe District and the Silver King Mine. Near Globe, however, he met a man who had just come from the Silver King and who informed him that Albert had gone to work at the McCracken Mine; this was located near the Bill Williams River in Mohave County in northwestern Arizona—some 250 to 300 miles from Globe.[6] Yet Schieffelin could go no further; his mules had thrown their shoes and had sore feet, he had no money for provisions, game was scarce in that vicinity, and he was hungry. What he needed was a temporary job. Thus he went into Globe seeking employment.

But there was no work to be had. He then went out to one of the mines, the McCullen, to ask for work; there at the company store he spent his last quarter for tobacco, and there also he met two men he had known in California who had been prospecting fruitlessly and who had turned to making adobe bricks to earn enough to eat while waiting for a job at the mines to open. He stayed the night with them, then the next morning talked to the foreman of the McCullen only to be informed that there was a long waiting list for employment. This discouraging news caused him to gather his mules and start back toward Globe although he had not a cent to his name. Three miles from town he passed the Champion Mine and fell in with a man bound for a nearby boarding house; naturally he asked about the possibilities of work at the Champion, inquiring if the foreman might hire him. The man with whom he was speaking replied that he was the foreman.

"I must have work," Schieffelin told him.

"Well," replied the foreman, "you can go to work at the windlass to-night, if that will suit you."

The windlass job was desperately hard work and the pay was only three dollars for the ten-hour night shift. Yet so great was Schieffelin's need that for the next fourteen nights he worked the windlass. This was in the open without shelter, and most of his pay was scrip good only at a certain store. This he used to purchase clothes and provisions and to have his mules shod. Then with seventy-five cents in his pocket he set out for the McCracken Mine to find Albert.

He traveled hard, going straight to his destination. He arrived there late at night, put his mules in the local corral, and then walked the nine miles to the mine before he could get anything to eat. At last he was reunited with his brother, whom he found working at the Signal Mine.[7] Ed did not blurt out his intentions to Al immediately, for he knew his brother was not given to enthusiasms or to be one easily excited about a new venture; in fact, Ed decided the best way to win over his brother was through gradualism. Meanwhile he would get a job and go to work, and this was the subject to which he addressed himself during their first conversation. The foreman, who was camping with Al near the mine, told Ed over a meal that he could go to work filling buckets on an eight-hour shift for four dollars a day. Ed therefore returned to town for his mules the next day, purchased a few necessities on credit, and returned to begin work that night at 11:00 p.m. at the Signal.

In the next several days Ed casually unfolded the story of his prospecting during the four years intervening since he last had seen Al. He told his brother and the foreman that he had been searching in the San Pedro country, that he thought he had found some promising samples, that he had shown these to people he had met on the trail north, but that these individuals, with but few exceptions, had told him the samples consisted mainly of lead—and thus were very poor. He went on to say that therefore he had thrown away most of his samples but that he still had three or four of the better pieces which he would show them and which he intended to have assayed. He concluded by stating that if the assay proved the samples poor, he intended to give up prospecting inasmuch as a poor assay would indicate he knew nothing about ore. Neither Al nor the foreman thought the samples of any value when Ed pulled them out and showed them. Therefore Ed worked quietly at the mine filling buckets for the next three weeks and more, helping his brother build a stone cabin during their free time and saying little. He had decided to wait for a propitious moment before pushing further.

At this juncture the company operating the Signal Mine employed the services of an assayer and sent him to the area to make tests on the ore coming from its properties. There the assayer erected a cabin and began working with his furnace and his tools. Thus the Schieffelins came into contact with Richard Gird, known as Dick. Gird was born at Litchfield, New York, on March 29, 1836. His common school education provided him with a good knowledge of trigonometry; however, his father, a dairy operator, held the motto of "work, work, work, and study, study, study" constantly before his children and young Gird read omnivorously. At the age of sixteen he left the family home for California where he became proficient at mining and where he studied the assayer's trade.

This knowledge he used to secure a job in 1858 which took him to Valparaiso, Chile, as a civil engineer. Two years later he returned to California by way of New York, and then in 1861 he came to Arizona, bringing with him what was rumored to be the first civil engineering and assaying outfit in the territory. With William D. Bradshaw he started a ferry across the Colorado River at the site of the future town of Ehrenberg, opening a road from there to Prescott in order to deliver freight. And they fought the Apaches and other tribes which sought to rob their caravans.

In 1864 the First Legislature of the Territory thought so highly of Gird's talents that it employed him to make a map of Arizona, a map that when completed was used for years by the army as well as by civil officials. Then for a time he moved to San Francisco where he was engaged in the manufacturing of mining machinery, but he returned to Arizona in 1874 to erect smelters and put them into operation. Thus late in 1877 he arrived at the Signal Mine, an experienced engineer and assayer, knowledgeable about mines and mining, and eager to make the fortune that so far had eluded him.[8]

That fall of 1877 Ed Schieffelin had never heard of Dick Gird, but Al had made his acquaintance previously. Thus it was Al who took three pieces of the Tombstone ore samples to Gird and asked that they be assayed, saying that he would pay for the work. Gird did the work on two of the samples, and then asked Al where the samples had come from. Al replied that he did not know specifically, only that his brother Ed had found them in the southern part of Arizona. With some enthusiasm doubtless showing in his voice, Gird—according to the way Ed later recalled the conversation—replied, "Well, the best thing you can do is to find out where that ore came from, and take me with you and start for the place."

Ed, who got off work at 7:00 a.m., was asleep in their cabin when Al returned from this conversation with Gird to get ready to go to work at 3:00 p.m. He awakened the sleeping Ed and told him the result of the assay: "That ore of yours, one piece goes $600 to the ton, and the other only $40." It later was revealed that the $40-to-the-ton ore was from the Tombstone claim recorded in Griffith's name. The other was from a claim which Ed had registered in his own name.

Gird also had told Al that he would do the assay on the third piece of ore the following day, so Ed made it a point to stop by personally to hear the result. When Gird finished, he asked Ed what he thought the third piece of ore showed. Ed replied he "thought about $1,000" to the ton. He was only half right. It had assayed at $2,000 to the ton—a fabulously rich piece of ore—and was from the Graveyard claim registered in Ed Schieffelin's name. Gird's next comment was to the effect that he would like to go to the San Pedro mines with the Schieffelins on a joint prospecting venture. Ed gave him no definite answer at the time, however, merely suggesting that the assayer come by the brothers' cabin some day and discuss the possibility.

The problem was that Al Schieffelin had as yet not agreed to go, and to this Ed addressed himself that evening. He told of Gird's assay of the third piece of ore and then point-blank asked Al if he would go to the Tombstone vicinity. Ed suggested that they quit their jobs at the Signal Mine and go together, the three of them, for they knew the ore was good and the location promising. Al replied that Gird was a good man and an excellent assayer—and thus would make as fine a partner as any man could want. This was not really an answer to Ed's question, and thus he pushed for something more definite, saying that Gird wanted to go and "will be around to talk about it in a few days, and I want to know what you think about it." Still Al was hesitant to join; he said that he was getting four dollars for an eight-hour shift at the Signal Mine and that he could not find a better job anywhere in the territory. There the matter rested "for a day or two."

When Gird did come to the Schieffelin's cabin, he was ready to talk seriously. He told the brothers that he could contribute an assaying outfit, that jointly they should purchase a wagon, that he could furnish one mule for it and Ed the other, and that together the three should go to the San Pedro area prepared to stay as long as they wanted. Ed's comment was that he had not been able to prospect the area sufficiently to satisfy himself when he was there the previous spring and summer and that he was certain rich mines could be found if he had both the time and an assayer who could give him an immediate indication of the true worth of the ores and float that he found. The session ended inconclusively, nonetheless, for Al still hung back. And Ed wanted him in on the venture rather than just himself and Gird going together.

The two brothers had a final session by themselves. At this meeting Ed restated Gird's offer and explained his conviction that riches were at Tombstone; he said that Al should not allow this opportunity to slip by, and he concluded by asking his brother to go, saying that he wanted him in the venture. Finally Al consented by saying, "All right, I will go."

To this Ed declared, "Let us go at once."

Immediately he went to tell Gird that the two were ready, and an agreement was made. They would be equal partners, share and share alike, but there would be no additional partners. Nothing was put in writing, for the three believed a handshake to be all they needed.

Once this agreement had been made and the partnership arranged, Ed was anxious to depart. Gird counseled waiting for spring; it then was January 1878 and snow was falling. "No," responded Ed, "I won't wait until spring; you may, but I shall go now, and you can come on in the spring." Ed's insistence caused the other two to agree but with strong reluctance. Still it was a month before they could leave, for Gird had business affairs to arrange, a mission on which he departed at once. This he completed on February 10, and the three men then began preparing to leave.

In this one-month interval rumors had begun to circulate in Signal City about the venture. Few of the miners there could understand why Gird would join a prospecting group, especially when he had been offered the general superintendency of the company operating the Signal Mine. The conclusion was obvious, and many of the miners in the vicinity reached it: the Schieffelins and Gird knew of a big location! Naturally these miners wanted to learn where it was so that they could participate in the initial location of rich claims. Frequently the three men were asked their destination as their preparations were observed, but Ed Schieffelin had anticipated such a reaction and had not told anyone, not even Al and Dick Gird, the exact spot where he had found his ore. Moreover, he constantly reminded his partners of the necessity of secrecy, for he was determined "to get to the mines first and have my choice of them."

On February 14 the three finally were ready to leave Signal City. Just at the moment of departure the whistle at one of the reduction works signaled noon, whereupon Gird and Al Schieffelin suggested they wait for lunch. However, Ed was in too great a frenzy of impatience even to want to eat; "I have been waiting long enough," he declared emphatically, "and we will go at once." Al mounted his saddle horse while Gird and Ed rode in the wagon, and they set out to cover the four hundred miles to their goal. Once on the road they learned from a stage-station operator that one party was ahead of them bound for the San Pedro Valley, a party composed of men from the vicinity of Signal City who had departed a few days earlier. Ed's fears of not being first to Tombstone increased when they reached Tucson and learned that this group of men was still a day ahead of them.

And that fear grew yet more as they followed the road east from the Old Pueblo. For forty miles they followed the tracks of the party in advance of them. Then at the point where the road forked, the main-traveled branch going on east to New Mexico and the other turning south to Tres Alamos and the Tombstone district, Schieffelin's fears became reality—for the men ahead of them had taken the south fork of the road. The two brothers and Gird hurried along the south branch of the road themselves. And to their delight they came to an abandoned stage station, there to see in the corral the wagons and mules of the party ahead of them. Later they would learn that one member of the party was inside the stage station but was too sick to come to the door; also, that another one of the group, a man named Parsons, was off prospecting in the Whetstone Mountains, that he knew Gird's reputation, and that he would have followed them had he been at the stage station when they passed.

Now almost in a feverish rush to get to their goal, the three partners hurried upriver, camped overnight, and then drove to within three miles of the Brunckow Mine. They intended to move

Ruins of the buildings at the Brunckow Mine; it was in these buildings that the Schieffelins and Gird lived while searching for silver at Tombstone. *Courtesy Arizona Historical Society.*

to an abandoned adobe house near that first mining effort in the San Pedro Valley, using it as their place of residence. But the road proved so rough that they halted and camped out yet another night; the next morning, leaving their wagon behind, they made their way on foot to the adobe hut. There they found that a party of miners had just left it for the Tombstone hills after writing their names on the walls of the structure. Inasmuch as the partners had heard that the Apaches temporarily were at peace, and thus that their hair probably would remain safely on their heads, they decided to move into the house and openly use it as their headquarters. The next day, February 26, they managed to move their wagon to this spot, unloaded it, and moved in. And the house proved ideal for their purposes. It contained two fireplaces, one of which they used for heating and cooking and the other of which became Gird's assay furnace.

The next day they established a regular routine. Gird, using some quartz samples, began running assay tests, while the Schieffelin brothers prospected for ore and float. Each morning they would leave Gird at the house doing his work, and each evening they would return with samples for him to assay the following day. Nothing exciting happened at first. Ed and Al were bringing in excellent samples of float which, when assayed, showed promise. In fact, some of it ran thousands of dollars to the ton. But they could not find the lode from which the float came—and the worm of fear and envy was eating inside them. They knew that the party from northern Arizona which had preceded them was somewhere in the vicinity, possibly near Apache Pass. Its members might find the lode first and the boys thus would miss out on the riches that would result. This thought, this fear, caused Gird to suggest, "If we do not find something in a day or two, let us pack up and go and see where those fellows have gone."

Ed Schieffelin considered this proposal overnight before rendering his decision, which was that he did not want to quit that location too hastily. In fact, he suggested that he take his mule and make a pass through the country hunting for ore, for he had privately decided that if he left Gird might change his mind about moving. Al seemed indifferent to the whole question, asking only if there was some operating mine in the vicinity where he could get work when the three of them quit their prospect.

"We will have something to work ourselves," Ed assured his brother. "Don't be uneasy about work."

"Well," replied his pragmatic brother, "we haven't got it yet."

Ed thereupon took his mule and departed. Actually he did no prospecting on this jaunt; rather he simply rode into the Dragoon Mountains and stayed gone overnight. As he was returning the following day, he passed over the exact spot where the city of Tombstone would grow, a flat area known as Goose Flats; simultaneously he was traversing the site of the Tough Nut Mine, although he did not know this at the time. This ride convinced him that he would stay no matter what his partners decided. Gird could leave and he would stay; Al likewise could leave and he would stay. He knew that riches were in the area, and he was going to stay until he found them.

He returned to the cabin after dark to find his two partners still there. But their two mules and Al's horse were gone. At first the three men feared that the Indians had stolen the animals, for they could find no tracks of humans around the corral, and their fears increased greatly; if renegades were in the vicinity, their work would be greatly hampered. All the next day they hunted the three missing animals, but with no result. Therefore on the day following that, Ed rode his mule to the river, a mile and a half away, crossed to the far side, and there found the animals' tracks; they were headed toward Tucson. He finally overtook the three reluctant pioneers some twelve miles away from the cabin, rounded them up, and drove them back—to the great relief of all three men, for the loss of these animals would have been serious indeed. Prospectors could not afford to be afoot in that country. But the best news to the men was that hostile Indians apparently were not in the region.

In the general letdown after this incident, nothing further was said about leaving the prospect. The next day Ed and Al set out as usual, leaving Gird behind to work at his assay furnace. However, they were out of meat, and thus it was necessary that either Al or Ed go hunting that day for a deer. Al proposed that the hunter should be Ed, saying that he would prospect at a spot they referred to as the Owl's Nest. However, Ed declined, stating that he could not kill anything that day; he was too excited about a piece of "very pretty ore" about the size of a hen's egg which he had found a few days before. It had assayed at $5000 to the ton and contained a large amount of gold. So Ed told his brother to hunt the deer while he tried to trace that piece of ore to its source.

That afternoon Al returned after a successful hunt—to find that Ed likewise had made a killing. He was building a monument, the usual way of staking a claim on the public domain before the discoverer could get to the nearest seat of government to record the title legally. Such a monument had binding validity in every western court of the day. When Ed saw his brother, he called him "to come and see what I had found, if he did not think there was rich ore in that country." Al looked on as Ed demonstrated just how rich was his find by striking the head of his pick down into the "rock." It went in easily, proving the ore to be extremely rich in silver.

"Yes, that is rich ore," Al agreed in what would prove to be an understatement. What Ed had found was an outcropping of ore six or seven inches wide and some forty to fifty feet long. In some places this ore was so nearly pure silver that they could press a half-dollar into it, pull it out, and see an exact mirror-image likeness of the coin left behind.

They finished building the monument before hurrying with samples back to their headquarters for Gird to assay. They did not need this testing to tell them that they had found good ore; rather they wanted an assay to tell them just how rich it was. As they entered the house, Ed told Gird excitedly, "I've got some rich ore this time."

The assayer replied that the ore Ed had found on his previous trip to that area had assayed at an incredible $6000 to $7000 to the ton. But Ed and Al brushed this aside as unimportant, demanding a quick assay of the new samples. When Gird completed this, he looked up to say, "Ed, you lucky cuss—you have hit it." Thereby he gave a name to the claim. The Lucky Cuss it was. The ore, said Gird, was worth $15,000 to the ton. Later tests would reveal that some of the ore from the Lucky Cuss carried $1200 to $1500 to the ton in gold along with $12,000 to $15,000 to the ton in silver.

A change instantly came over all three at this moment, Ed Schieffelin later recalled, for they realized that their dream had come true. His especially, for it was he who had believed they would find rich mines in the Tombstone area. It had been his faith and his perseverance more than anything else which had brought the three men there and which had kept them there. Now their problem was to locate the richest mines and stake them before others cashed in on their discovery and beat them to the best bodies of ore.

The next morning all three men went to the Lucky Cuss to refine the claim that Ed and Al had staked the day before. They built additional monuments and took more ore samples. At one large outcropping in the area of their claims, Gird took a chunk from one side and then moved thirty feet to the other side for an additional sample; the following day, after he had assayed the two pieces of ore, he announced that they were the best samples he had ever taken in his life considering the width of the ledge. Ed Schieffelin would later recall of that day, "We were now all perfectly satisfied that we had found all we wanted."[9]

But finding the ore body was only part of the process of getting wealthy. The three men had been prospecting and mining sufficiently long to know that the discovery often proved the easiest problem to solve. Before they could reap the reward for their effort, they had to keep the discovery a secret until they could file a claim at the County Recorder's Office; the Tombstone District was at the time located in Pima County, which meant a journey to Tucson, the county seat. Then when their claims had been registered, they would have to decide whether they wanted to sell out to some capitalist who could furnish the large capital outlay necessary for a mining operation based on hard-rock ore, or whether they wished to try to raise the money themselves and go into the mining business themselves. Making their discovery pay dividends would be an involved undertaking, one requiring a large sum of money and great technical know-how.

They had found the ore. Now came the hard work of developing the mines.

Developing the Mines

The immediate, pressing, and overriding task for the partners, Ed and Al Schieffelin and Dick Gird, once they had found their bonanza strike, was to prevent its being stolen. Already a swarm of prospectors was moving into the region as rumors circulated that riches were to be had in the San Pedro Valley. Many intuitive men seemed to sense that Tombstone's time had come. Nor were such men entirely honest. For example, the Schieffelins and Gird noticed just a day after their big discovery that a strange burro was in the corral with their animals, but the next night it was gone. A check revealed tracks of the person who had come to take the animal away. Moreover, there were tracks leading to the window of their building, the window where Gird set his assay samples to cool after they had been heated in the furnace.

Within two days of these disturbing incidents, two men walked into the partners' camp, Hank Williams and John Oliver. Gird saw them first and opened a conversation with them. To his questions about their intentions, they replied that they had come to prospect. Ed Schieffelin saw them next; he was returning from a trek in the hills and found the two newcomers camped at the spring where the partners had been getting their water. From them he learned that they had made an agreement with Gird, who was to do their assays in return for their making a joint location should they discover anything (a joint location meant that two claims would be made at the point of discovery, one party to build the monument and the other to have the first choice of the two resulting claims). And Gird kept his part of the bargain, thereafter assaying whatever samples the two newcomers brought in.

It was at this time that Ed Schieffelin made yet another spectacular find. He and Al continued their hunting, and one morning he started out from the original ledge, the Lucky Cuss, to try to ascertain just which way the ledge ran when it ran underground. A mining claim was only 600 by 1500 feet, and naturally prospectors wanted to be as certain as possible that they recorded within this limit the richest ore; but when the ore ran underground, this often proved difficult. From the Lucky Cuss, Ed moved northwest, relying on experience—and intuition—to tell him which way the underground ledge ran. For a mile and a half he walked up a gulch; there he found rich float, which in turn he traced up yet another gulch. And there he discovered a ledge, the same one, he hoped, that went underground at the Lucky Cuss. Quickly he erected a monument claiming it for himself, his brother, and Dick Gird. Later, in telling them of his find, he commented that tracing the underground ledge had been a tough nut to crack; thereby he gave a name to the new claim, which would be known as the Tough Nut Mine.

The same day that Ed was locating the Tough Nut, Hank Williams, one of the two newcomers, was deciding to leave the region. He was discouraged inasmuch as the richest ore he had brought to Gird for assay had shown only seventy dollars to the ton. This was not enough to make mining profitable. Williams' problem was that he believed silver would be found only in connection with black iron outcroppings in that region. Later he would be proven correct, for silver was found in this way—but underground where Williams, with his limited resources, was unable to locate it. And the same day that Ed was in the hills tracing the ledge up to the Tough Nut, Al Schieffelin and Dick Gird were preparing to go to

Tucson for provisions. Williams thus decided to leave the San Pedro Valley in their company, departing the region for good. But Gird gave him encouragement, saying he would strike it rich yet if he but had patience and perseverance. Williams was gradually converted to sufficient optimism to agree to stay yet a while longer.

It was on that evening that Ed returned to camp with ore samples from his new discovery, the Tough Nut. These later proved to be very rich in horn silver; when Gird assayed them, he found the samples worth $2200 to the ton. The next day Ed was returning to the Tough Nut area for yet more samples, and on the way he overtook Williams, who also was going into the hills. Perhaps feeling sorry for the unfortunate prospector, Ed showed him the samples of his newest discovery, then continued on to the Tough Nut to try to ascertain the exact direction of the ledge when it went underground at that site. For a week he worked at this puzzle, by which time he was ready for a change of pace. At this point his brother and Gird returned from Tucson, and the three men decided to build a cabin at the site of the Lucky Cuss claim; such a move would protect them against claim-jumpers. Thus Ed stopped his prospecting in favor of saw and hammer and adobe bricks.

But Williams continued to prospect—and found the Grand Central Mine, which would prove the richest find in the entire district. It was only a mile from the Tough Nut. However, Williams did not make a joint location, which he had agreed to do when he first arrived and asked Gird to run his assays for him. He had made only one claim, one which encompassed the entire ledge he had discovered. Naturally the partners wanted to share in this discovery, and they visited Williams at his camp. An argument quickly erupted.

"Haven't I kept my part of the agreement . . . ?" asked Gird.

Williams replied that the assayer had, but said he nevertheless was going to keep his find for himself. After lengthy discussion, however, he did agree to slice off the western portion of the ledge and give it to the partners. This they took, calling it the Contention as a result of the way in which they had acquired it. But it left such a sour taste in Ed Schieffelin's mouth that he was ready to stop prospecting. Besides, said he, the best claims already had been located, a view which time proved correct. The Grand Central, the Contention, and the Tough Nut would prove to be the three major properties in the Tombstone District, while the Lucky Cuss would prove to be only a small pocket of ore and thus a disappointment.

Shortly after this distasteful quarrel with Williams, yet another newcomer arrived at the partners' cabin, a distant relative of Dick Gird, Thomas Walker. He also had been employed at the Signal Mine in northwestern Arizona, but he had not been asked into the partnership. When Gird and the Schieffelins departed for the San Pedro Valley, however, he decided to follow them. He made this decision solely on the basis of Gird's reputation, for he believed Gird would not leave for southern Arizona without strong evidence of a potential bonanza. And following the three men proved very easy; he set out in the same direction they had taken and then asked about them at every stage station along the road until he reached the area they were in.

For several weeks Walker remained with the three men. He spent his time tramping the hills hunting for a prospect, while Gird did his assay work for him. But he found nothing. Just as he had become sufficiently discouraged to talk of leaving, Gird spoke to Ed Schieffelin of the possibility of giving his relative one of the partners' claims. Ed agreed, for they had one claim that had been located only with a monument but which they had put no other work into. That evening Gird took Walker to this site and changed the name on the location notice to Walker's name; because of the time of day when they arrived, Walker decided to call the site the Sunset Mine. And the next day, Ed Schieffelin left for Tucson where he gratuitously recorded the mine in Walker's name. This claim, which had cost Walker exactly nothing, he would later sell for $25,000—it was an expensive gift for the partners to give away.

Walker did not realize the need for secrecy. Shortly after he acquired title to the mine, he took samples from it to Fort Huachuca where he showed them, creating excitement—and starting a rush to Tombstone. By this time, however, two of the original three partners had also passed word to others. Gird and Al Schieffelin had written letters to friends at the Signal Mine telling of their discoveries and urging these old acquaintances to hurry to the region before all the good locations were made. Thus other men started arriving in the Tombstone District.

And that first party which the partners had outdistanced, that of Smith, White, and Parsons, finally found the mineral district. They had turned into Guadalupe Canyon to the north (near Fort Apache), but had found it barren of promise. Thus eventually, by a process of elimination, they came into the area. Learning that Gird was there, they came to the Lucky Cuss where they talked with Walker and Al Schieffelin, Gird and Ed Schieffelin being in Tucson at the time. When those two returned, it was to learn that already Smith had become discouraged after fruitless prospecting and had departed for Mexico. But White and Parsons remained. They also were searching without result, whereupon they finally approached the partners about purchasing some of their properties.

The Schieffelins and Gird did need money to continue working their claims until major financing could be arranged. Thus after some discussion they agreed to sell Parsons and White the Tough Nut for $50,000 and the Contention for $20,000. After lengthy haggling about price, White and Parsons offered $10,000 for the Contention. This the partners finally decided to accept inasmuch as they had not done any work on that particular site; nor did the Contention show any real promise except for some good float on the surface. Cursory digging had revealed some fair croppings two or three feet underground, but the potential seemed so poor that they were willing to sell it. Thus in April 1878 a contract was made; White and Parsons were to have eighty days in which to go to San Francisco and raise the $10,000, after which they were to open the mine immediately and begin work. The intent here, of course, was that a successful opening of the Contention would help the partners in getting other financing. White did leave for San Francisco immediately after signing the contract, the money was raised, the partners were paid, and work did begin at the Contention.

The news of this sale, when reported in newspapers in Arizona and California, added to the exciting talk and rumor that was current about Tombstone. Yet more prospectors arrived, along with a flurry of financial manipulations. Oliver Jacobs came to the three partners, saying he had been referred to them by Charles Tozier of Tucson; he wanted to examine their claims with the possibility of purchasing one or more of them. After his checking, he returned to ask the three men to name a price. Gird and the Schieffelins offered him the Tough Nut and two or three nearby claims for $50,000 and the Lucky Cuss and its nearby claims for $40,000. Jacobs said he would buy them at that price provided they tested satisfactorily; he did want independent assays to assure himself that the claims had not been salted. All final arrangements were to be made by Tozier. Jacobs then took samples with him and departed.

Soon Isaac E. "Ike" James arrived from San Francisco to make the evaluation for Jacobs. James had been hired for this task because of his reputation as an engineer; he was widely known in the West by members of the mining fraternity for his work at the Comstock Lode of Nevada where he had made the earliest maps of the famous Ophir Mine and others.[1] He was later described as genial, intelligent, and charming, but his chore in 1878 was as a consultant; thus he poked about, took samples which he assayed, and then made his report. It was so favorable that a contract of sale was drawn between the partners and Tozier (on behalf of Jacobs). This contract gave Jacobs a first option to purchase the claims within sixty days, for which he paid a deposit fee. But by the expiration of that first date, July 2, Jacobs and his financiers had not delivered the $90,000. They requested an extension of the deadline, which the partners granted, extending the due date to August 1 on condition of $100 per day forfeit. Again the deadline came and went, and the contract expired. The money forfeited by Jacobs, together with what the partners had realized from the sale of the Contention, totaled some $15,000. This sum enabled them to continue developing their claims and to wait for the arrival of the big money men—which occurred in September that year, 1878.

The financial arrangements that enabled the partners to develop the claims and to realize their potential originated from one of the trips that had been made to Tucson to secure supplies. In March, when Al Schieffelin and Dick Gird went to the Old Pueblo to record the initial claims at the Pima County Recorder's Office, they also had visited Tucson gun dealer John Selah Vosburg to propose a grubstaking arrangement. The partners had said originally that they would have no additional men involved in their venture, but by March they were so short of finances that they needed help. Thus they went to Vosburg, who was known to invest occasionally in a prospecting venture. In this he was not unique; the mining fever had infected almost everyone in Arizona, and those who could not go personally could at least participate vicariously by investing a few dollars here and there. In return for a few dollars advanced by some businessman or for a few supplies furnished by a merchant, the prospector agreed to split a specified percentage of the proceeds of his discovery or else to make a joint location. Generally these arrangements were verbal in nature, but the practice was so well known that they were legally binding in the courts of mining states in the West.

John Vosburg was no stranger to this practice. A native of western New York State, he had come to Tucson in December 1869 to establish a business as a dealer in arms and ammunition. In Arizona he had prospered both in business and in politics. He had served in the House of Representatives of the Seventh Legislative Assembly in 1873, a representative of his home town of Tucson; and in 1877 he was appointed territorial auditor by Governor A. P. K. Safford. Moreover, he and Safford were secretly partners for purposes of making investments in mining properties. Anson

A. P. K. Safford, former governor of Arizona Territory who was a silent partner of John Vosburg and "grubstaked" the discovery of the Tombstone District by the Schieffelins and Dick Gird. *Courtesy Arizona Historical Society.*

Peacely-Killen Safford, Arizona's third territorial governor, was a native of Vermont who had worked in the gold fields of California and Nevada. In 1867 he had been named surveyor general of Nevada, a position he held until April 7, 1869, when President Ulysses S. Grant named him governor of Arizona. In this capacity he served for eight years, the longest span of any of Arizona's seventeen territorial governors, proving himself to be an excellent and innovative chief executive in several respects. During his years as governor, "Little Saff," as he was known, tried to increase his private fortune by investing in various mining ventures, just as he worked hard to improve the public fortunes of the territory. Naturally his financial investments had to be done in secret, and for this purpose he approached John Vosburg. By 1878, when Safford no longer was governor and even had returned to the East, the two men had lost $12,000 in their investments—but not their enthusiasm.

Thus when Al Schieffelin and Dick Gird approached the gun dealer to become a partner with them and Ed Schieffelin, they unknowingly were adding yet a fifth name, that of ex-Governor Safford, to those that would profit from the transaction. As Vosburg later recalled the incident that led to his enrichment, he said, "Some people came into my place one day, rather diffident,—asked if I was Mr. Vosburg. I said, 'Yes.' Are you a friend of Governor Safford? Yes. They did not ask for family history showing that your grandfather came over in the Mayflower."

Gird's mention of Governor Safford's name was no accident. Earlier, when he had been working in the territory, he had met the governor, who had told him if he ever needed money to finance a mining venture to go to Vosburg. "We would like to say something to you; would you mind shutting the door?" Gird said that day in March 1878.

Vosburg did as requested, even taking the precaution of locking the door to his business. Al and Gird then forthrightly told the gun dealer that they were prospectors and said they had reason to believe that riches might be found in the Chiricahua Mountains. This was a deliberate lie about the true location of their discoveries, but naturally they were cautious previous to reaching a definite agreement. Gird then explained that Safford had told him to come to Vosburg should he need supplies; he did not know that Safford had told Vosburg also to furnish reasonable aid should Gird come to him. Gird and Schieffelin concluded by stating that they wanted to be out for another month, although perhaps a shorter period of time would suffice, and for this they needed some supplies.

Vosburg asked them how much they needed.

They responded that they wanted goods totaling $200 to $250. Without another word Vosburg unlocked his door and escorted the two men personally across the street to the firm of Lord and Williams, one of the largest mercantile firms in Tucson and southern Arizona. Inside he told the proprietor that Gird and Schieffelin wanted supplies. "They will tell you what they want," he said. "I will be security for the amount of three hundred dollars for them." This would prove to be the most rewarding investment Vosburg would make in his life.

Gird and Al Schieffelin spent that night and the next at Vosburg's establishment. He offered them his own bed, which was in his shop, but they said they preferred to sleep on the ground. Then they slipped out of town during the hours of darkness. Ten days later Gird was back, this time to suggest that Vosburg personally should locate some claims in the San Pedro Valley, for the strike had been made. The gun dealer responded that he knew nothing about mining but that he would help the partners raise the capital they needed to develop their find. And he was as good as his word: he wired east to Safford, "These men have reason to think they have found something. Lightning don't strike but once in one place." And, according to his reminiscence of these events, Vosburg kept the pressure on Safford to hurry; repeatedly he telegraphed, "The boys report it looks fine! looks fine!"

Safford had been in Arizona long enough to realize the potential of a big strike, and he contacted Eastern capitalists who might want to invest, specifically Phillip Corbin and his brother George, owners of the Corbin House Hardware Company of New Britain, Connecticut. Moreover, Safford came to the Tombstone site personally in September 1878, one month after the option with Tozier had expired, bringing with him Dan Gillette, yet another financier. Gillette, after inspecting the area, wanted to purchase the partners' claims outright for $150,000; at least this was the amount he implied they could get if they would sell to him. By this time, however, the Schieffelins and Gird had a sounder appreciation of the true worth of their holdings, and thus they refused the offer.

Then the Corbin brothers came to the territory, bringing with them Dr. Cox, the state geologist of Indiana. The Corbins had heard horror stories of Eastern investors being swindled by wily prospectors, and they wanted an independent and reliable examination made of the site by an outsider. From Tucson this party traveled to Tombstone in a leisurely fashion, taking Vosburg with them in a Concord coach drawn by five horses and with a special driver; it took them two weeks to make this trip, for they toured the Oro Blanco District, the Patagonia Mountains, site of mining activity in the 1850s, and the Harshaw Mountains. Once at the site, Dr. Cox began his investigation. The Schieffelins took him on a complete tour of their claims, even down into the shafts they already had sunk. In the two or three hours required for Cox's survey, Vosburg led Safford aside to the top of the little hill where they could get a panoramic view of the area. "Governor," said Vosburg earnestly, "it is right here! *Now Lightning has struck!* . . . They have got the kale seed! I can get ore—horn silver—that will assay thirty thousand." Vosburg wanted to consummate the deal as fast as possible.

And Dr. Cox's report to the Corbin brothers confirmed Vosburg's optimism. The geologist said that in the different claims which he had checked was silver to the value of at least $2,500,000. This satisfied the Corbins, and an agreement was soon negotiated. George Corbin bought an interest in the Lucky Cuss and its related claims, these to be incorporated under the name the Corbin Mill and Mining Company. The Tough Nut and its related claims were to be incorporated under the name the Tombstone Milling and Mining Company. In return the Corbins were to raise up to $80,000, to be placed at Gird's disposal; all money spent in excess of $40,000 had to be repaid, however, with interest to date from the time the money was advanced and to be repaid from the first proceeds from the mines.

Each of the partners shared in the two new corporations. Ed and Al Schieffelin and Dick Gird each received a quarter interest; Vosburg and Safford shared a one-eighth interest; and the Corbins received a one-eighth interest. Moreover, all were to share in the water rights pertaining to the claims as well as in the townsite company to be formed. This agreement was signed in Tucson by all the interested parties, including ex-Governor Safford who thus publicly acknowledged his investment with Vosburg.

And each of these men had a share of work in getting the corporations into production. Governor Safford and Al Schieffelin departed for the East to sell stock in the companies; this they did at Philadelphia and other cities, thereby raising the funds necessary for purchasing machinery, hiring workers, and starting the mines. The Corbins left $1000 in an account with Vosburg for incidental expenses before they likewise departed for the East, there to aid in raising money. Dick Gird left for San Francisco, where at the Fulton Iron Works he superintended the construction of a ten-stamp mill. When it was completed, he oversaw its packing and transportation to Tombstone.

John Vosburg's part was to move to the San Pedro River to construct a dam that would raise the level of the water twelve feet. Also, he was to oversee the construction of flumes to carry water to the mill site, a vital necessity for the operation of a stamp mill. While this construction was under way, the gun dealer lived in a Sibley tent, camping on the banks of the river; the site he selected was where a large stand of cottonwoods provided shade. He also was planning and laying out the foundation for the ten-stamp mill.

And while Gird was in San Francisco at the Fulton Iron Works, he paused in his work there long enough to purchase a portable saw mill. This he sent by ship, which sailed from San Francisco around the tip of Baja California and up the Gulf of California; at the mouth of the Colorado River, it was transferred to steamboat for movement to Fort Yuma. Unloaded there, it was taken on big wagons under the direction of Ham Light, transported to Tucson, and from there it was sent to the Huachuca Mountains, twelve miles from the stamp mills. It was reassembled and on January 14, 1879, commenced to operate; thereafter its operators, John McCloskey and William K. Gird, kept a steady stream of timbers pouring from it. Its capacity was supposedly 10,000 board feet a day, but it produced only 6000 to 8000 board feet per day and did so with great difficulty.

Ed Schieffelin meanwhile had been in charge of work gangs that were constructing a road over which ore wagons would haul the output of the mines to the site of the mill. At last came Gird's arrival with the mill. He shipped it by way of the Southern Pacific Railroad, whose tracks had been completed to Fort Yuma; from that point the bulky and heavy mill was brought by wagons the 300 miles to the site on the banks of the San Pedro River nine miles from Tombstone. At the site of the foundation provided by Vosburg, the mill was erected along with other company buildings. One large, commodious structure was built to serve as the company headquarters. On the north side was the directors' room, the secretary's office, and an assay office. And in the assay office was a large vault in which the bullion from the mill could be stored in safety until it was transported to Tucson and deposited in the bank. This vault was constructed of quarter-inch wrought iron and contained what was described as a "burglar proof door."

On the south side of this building were bedrooms and a dining room. Through the center, running east and west, was a spacious hall, and a broad veranda surrounded the entire building. This structure was located between the Tombstone and Corbin mills on a small hill of fifty to seventy-five feet in elevation; thus from the west side of the building the resident or visitor could get a fine view of the San Pedro Valley, as well as see the mills turning out silver bullion. A correspondent for the *Arizona Daily Star* noted of the site, "The air is pure and pleasant and little or none of the sickness so prevalent in the valley need be feared. This structure, like the mill, which is also Gird's work, shows excellent judgment and taste in the design."[2]

Nearby, as indicated, the Corbin Mill and Mining Company's mill was being erected, but with considerably more difficulty. The site selected for it proved to be solid rock, and it cost the company $20,000 just to excavate the foundation; this rock likewise slowed the grading work. The mill itself was built by the Fulton Foundry of San Francisco, as was the mill under Gird's supervision, and was shipped to Tombstone in the same way. It was a fifteen-stamp mill, steam driven, and was ready to begin crushing ore on January 17, 1880—some six months after the Tombstone Mill and Mining Company's mill began operating.[3]

In preparation for the moment when Gird would order the process to begin, Ed Schieffelin at the Tough Nut began hiring miners to bring out the ore. For them the company erected a small store near the entrance to the mine to supply the miners' wants—at a profit, naturally. Food cost these men approximately a dollar a day, while their shelter was free; they simply built shanties of whatever materials were at hand, or else they erected tents with which to protect themselves from the weather.

As Schieffelin began hiring, he found little competition for labor. The famed Comstock mines of Nevada were declining rapidly at this time, as were the "glory holes" of many other localities. Thus hordes of unemployed miners were drifting into the San Pedro Valley, most of them Cornishmen familiarly known as "Cousin Jacks." In addition, there were many Irishmen, and there were ordinary Americans, some of whom were refugees from the oil fields of Pennsylvania. They were attracted by the top wages being paid at Tombstone, four dollars a day for a ten-hour shift; men who sank the shafts received six dollars a day, but their work was considerably more hazardous.

Miners at work in the Tombstone Consolidated Mines. Note the candles in the wall providing light. *Courtesy Arizona Historical Society.*

Actually a miner needed little excuse to come to the new camp, for many of them were vagabonds at heart. He went to see each new "elephant" (an expression of the day which had originated with P. T. Barnum's introduction of the circus elephant; "to see the elephant" meant to satisfy one's curiosity). He might take a job for a day, a week, a month, or longer, and then he would leave for no better reason than finding a lump in his morning oatmeal or because the morning's hotcakes were "out-of-round." His clothing was so universal that it was almost a uniform. On his head was a battered felt hat with a wide brim; this he stiffened with resin until it almost constituted a safety helmet, one capable of deflecting light blows. A short-sleeved undershirt, union drawers, a shirt of heavy weave, baggy trousers always appearing about to fall off, and boots or ankle-high brogans were standard dress, although when working under extremely wet conditions he would dress like a sailor in a sou'wester and oilskins.

There were two ten-hour shifts working around the clock in the mines. The four surplus hours allowed each crew one hour coming to work and another going. At the start of a shift the crew would first muck out the ore left by the blast of the preceding crew. That sent to the surface, the men then began drilling holes for new blasts. This was done in two-man teams, one holding the steel drilling rod and the other man sledging it with an eight-pound double jack. As the drill was struck, the man holding would turn it to get a uniformly round hole. When the man sledging became tired, he changed places with his partner. In this way they could progress into granite at the rate of one-fifth inch per hour, faster when cutting into softer material. Their light for this work was given by candles, generally jammed into the wall of the tunnel facing in a candle holder; inasmuch as a candle of the usual length burned more than three hours, each man was issued three of them as he descended for his shift.

As the end of a shift approached, the men prepared to set their charges. For this purpose the blaster prepared paper cartridges, generally above ground to use natural light rather than risk the danger of premature ignition of the powder by candle fire. These cartridges were driven into the holes, then were tamped with damp clay; this was a delicate art inasmuch as too much clay left too little room for powder, while too little clay allowed the shot to blow most of its force out of the hole and not blast loose the ore. The blaster then yelled "Fire in the hole!" to warn the men that he was lighting the fuses; then he departed at a walking pace. To run was to risk stumbling or else to be knocked unconscious by an unseen obstruction. Then the men would emerge from their underground labors—smelling like the mine mules that pulled the ore carts, for they were covered with sweat, dust, and drip.[4]

Ed Schieffelin was living no better than his men when this operation started at the Tough Nut. His quarters likewise consisted of a tent, and he was below ground as often as above. The one concession which he and his partners granted to their miners was to furnish their clothing for the work in the mines. For paternalistic reasons this was not done. As a shift came out of the tunnels, the men had to shed their clothing, and Ed (or occasionally Gird) would inspect them to look for concealed nuggets. "They looked in our ears, noses, under our arms to see if we were carrying any metal," David Pitts later recalled of his stint at the Tough Nut in 1878. Just twenty-one years old at the time, Pitts did note that the partners had a good reason for checking the men so closely: "There were chunks of gold uncovered on the rocks after a blast." Naturally some of the men would try to steal the richest nuggets. Pitts concluded, "Tombstone sure was a bad town. I didn't stay very long. . . ."[5]

Once the ore was out of the ground, it had to be transported by wagon to the mill. These ore wagons were huge affairs, about half as big as a Pullman railroad car, and were drawn by mule teams of sixteen to twenty animals hitched in pairs. The cost was $3.50 per ton for transporting the ore just nine miles, but so much ore was shipped this way that scores of teamsters found employment in the Tombstone District. It was hot, dusty, boring work as the men swore at their animals, cracked their whips, wiped the swirling dust-mixed-with-sweat from their faces, and cursed the luck that had brought them to southern Arizona, but it paid well —and was not nearly so dangerous as working below ground.

The first load of ore arrived at Gird's mill on June 1, 1879, and nervously the partners watched as the process began. The first run through the mill was with third-class ore taken from Cross-Cut No. 1 at the Tough Nut; this poor ore was used first in order to fill all the cracks in the mill thoroughly before the high-grade ore was sent through. The water came through its ditch from the dam at the San Pedro, a structure 200 feet long about one mile from the mill; near the mill the water came through a flume measuring 4½ by 2½ feet, entered the iron penstock, and then dropped straight down 40 feet into a turbine wheel, turning this at the rate of 300 revolutions per minute. Thus the water provided power

A team of ore wagons showing how the ore was transported from the mines to the mill. *Courtesy Arizona Historical Society.*

for the mill, after which it entered a tailrace of 470 feet that carried it back to the San Pedro River.

The incoming ore was fed into and broken by the rock-breaker, which could crush quartz as fast as a man could shovel into it. From the rock-breaker, the crushed ore fell into batteries where it was pounded yet finer—until it would pass through a forty-mesh screen (forty meshes to the inch). Next it went to pans where, together with quicksilver, it was ground still finer; then it was taken to the settle where the "amalgam," as the mixture then was called, was allowed to set. When the amalgam was thick enough, it was taken to the "retort," and the tailings sent outside. At the Tombstone Milling and Mining Company operation, the usual run was expected to be from twelve to fifteen tons of amalgam in a twenty-four-hour period. The retort heated this mixture until the quicksilver turned to vapor (to escape through a pipe where water cooled it, it returned to the form of quicksilver, and was ready for use again; only a small part of it was lost in each run).

A view of Tombstone from the Grand Central Mill. *Courtesy Arizona Historical Society.*

The residue that was left behind was, as the miners said, "born into bullion" at this stage.

One of the workers in this operation, Sam Aaron, wrote of his experience thirty years later. He stated that his first job was to shovel ore into the rock-breaker. His first day's labor netted him $3.50, but he was so unaccustomed to the hard work that he could neither close nor straighten his hands when the day ended. Yet Aaron was a hard worker and soon advanced to the position of night boss, and even was offered the job of maintaining the furnaces; but he preferred not to work there, for the furnacemen were exposed to arsenic and lead poisoning. There reportedly was a doctor at Park City, Utah, who could cure the poisoning, but few furnacemen had the funds to travel there. But they found a way to get relief: they placed a loop of rope around their necks and legs, laid a pillow on their stomachs, and pulled tightly. This reportedly made them feel better, but they died just the same.

Aaron also told of how deadly were the volatile tempers of the men with whom he worked. On one occasion, as he recalled it, a feeder and chargewheeler got into a fight wherein the feeder hit the chargewheeler with a shovel, knocking the man unconscious; the feeder then shoved the unconscious man into the furnace and pitched his lunch bucket in behind him. This left behind no evidence of crime on which he could be tried. Eight months later the feeder became ill and, convinced that he was dying, he confessed his murder. Aaron concluded his reminiscence of work in the mill by stating, "the first opportunity I had . . . I started to be a faro-dealer."[6]

To the Schieffelins, Gird, Vosburg, and the other partners in this venture, the five days consumed by the first run of ore "seemed to drag slowly by." At least, that was how John Vosburg later described it: "We awoke frequently at night to listen to the lullaby of the stamps and never grumbled once—and then slept again with golden dreams."

At last came the moment all had been waiting for, the pouring of the first bar of bullion. Out it came, one bar tapering slightly at the ends, a mass of silver weighing eighty pounds. Gird followed the usual procedure for testing bullion: he took a chip off each side and the top and the bottom for assay; these he averaged in order to arrive at the purity and content of the bar. His work completed, he announced that the run had produced 4 per cent gold; the rest of it was pure silver. With the value of silver then ninety-eight cents an ounce, that first bar of bullion had a value of $18,064. The company directors were so pleased that they announced a dividend of $50,000 per month, a dividend that would be paid regularly for the next twenty-seven months without interruption.[7]

This silver had to be transported to Tucson for deposit in a bank, and that task fell to Ed Schieffelin because the stage lines then in operation between Tombstone and Tucson would not take the silver for fear of robbery. He loaded that first week's output on the same wagon in which he, Al, and Gird had first made their way from the Signal Mine to southern Arizona. When he arrived safely at the Old Pueblo, the silver was paraded through the town with hundreds of people turning out to get a look. A week later Schieffelin was back with a second load valued at $18,395.28 for deposit in the Safford Hudson Bank in Tucson; for this trip he had purchased a thoroughbrace wagon and a new span of mules. The newspaper account of this second arrival stated that the mill was running night and day.[8] Thereafter, Schieffelin regularly arrived in Tucson with the bullion each week. He took the precaution of hiring four men to help him; one man drove, two rode in the wagons as guards, and one man rode in front, another behind. Such was the mode of transportation until November 1879 when one of the stage lines finally agreed to accept responsibility for transporting the bullion for them.[9]

At this point, November 1879, Ed Schieffelin had become heartily dissatisfied with the role he had assumed as a businessman. He longed to return to the life of a prospector, and thus he left Gird and Al to run the company. Gathering an outfit, he fled into the hills to hunt for yet another bonanza. The wanderlust had struck him in direct proportion to the number of people settling in the area to mine—and the number was growing rapidly.

By the summer of 1879, when Schieffelin arrived in Tucson with the first bullion shipment, the Tombstone District was a hotbed of activity. The Tucson *Arizona Daily Star* of October 29, 1879, stated that the road between the two towns was lined with conveyances of every description "from the miner with his Arizona coat of arms, the burro, to the heavy teams all bound for the new Eldorado." It also noted that there were many locations, monuments, and prospect holes in the district, while Tucson newspapers were filled with accounts of the sale of several of the smaller mines at Tombstone. Even the far-off *Chicago Tribune*, as early as January 5, 1879, had commented, "In a few months the discovery of Tombstone put Arizona on the map and caused a rush like that of early Nevada and Colorado."

Another indication of the rapid settlement of the Tombstone District and of the heady rush to locate claims came from J. A.

Hoisting works at the Tough Nut Mine. *Courtesy Arizona Historical Society.*

Rockfellow, who had been living in Signal City when the Schieffe-lins and Gird were there. Rockfellow later recalled that Gird had written friends at Signal of the discovery and invited them to come down and participate. Rockfellow was one of those who started for Tombstone but was "sidetracked" by several jobs and thus did not arrive at the booming city in the San Pedro Valley until January 1881—at which time he asserted that he met four-fifths of the former population of Signal City now living at Tombstone.[10]

At first there were only a few mining companies. The rest of the properties were held by individual prospectors and investors. However, the holdings gradually would be consolidated into several large companies, for huge capital investments were necessary to make the hard-rock ore yield its bullion. This money came from the East—New York and Philadelphia—and from the West—Los Angeles and San Francisco. Few Arizonans possessed sufficient money to invest in smelting works, and thus the silver and gold produced at Tombstone did not remain in the territory except in the form of wages. And the production was huge. By 1881 there were more than 3000 claims located, but only 14 of the mines were equipped with complete hoisting works; by this same date there were mills with a combined total of 140 stamps in operation, and from them was coming half a million dollars monthly in bullion.[11]

The three leading companies were the Contention Consolidated, The Grand Central, and the Tombstone Mill and Mining Company. The most famous individual mines were the Tough Nut, the Contention, the Grand Central, the Head Center, and the Vizinia. The richest single mine in the camp was the one sold by the partners for only $10,000—the Contention. Owned by the Contention Consolidated Company, it, in fact, was the most productive in Arizona. This company was first incorporated in 1880 as the Western Mining Company; toward the end of 1881, however, it had consolidated with the Flora Morrison Mine and the Sulphuret, and the name was then changed to the Contention Consolidated Company. In 1882 this company extracted 25,017 tons of ore, produced 632 bars of silver valued at $1,676,795.96, and employed an average of 110 men to labor in its more than twenty miles of workings. By 1883 the company had produced more than $5,000,000 in bullion.[12]

The Grand Central Company was headquartered in Youngstown, Ohio. It owned and controlled such mines as the Grand Central, the Leviathan, the Naumkeag, the South Extension, the Emerald, the Moonlight, and the Grand Dipper, along with many lesser properties. By March 1881 it had produced $2,893,742.65, while the better-known Tombstone Mill and Mining Company from its eleven claims would extract $2,870,787.12 by 1883. The Vizinia was a New York corporation which worked the mine of the same name. Other lesser corporations included the Arizona Queen, a Boston corporation; the Lima Consolidated Mining Company of San Francisco; the Boston and Arizona and the

Mountain Maid, also of San Francisco; and the Bunker Hill, Mammoth, and Rattlesnake, which were owned in Chicago.

Accurate figures for the total output of the Tombstone mines are difficult to secure. Patrick Hamilton, writing about the resources of Arizona in 1883, estimated the total value of gold and silver taken from Tombstone during the first four years of mining there at $25,000,000. W. P. Blake in 1902 produced a far more conservative figure—one probably closer to the truth; he guessed the output as of January 1882 at $7,359,000, with dividends totaling more than $3,000,000.[13]

As inevitably happened in the American West when a large mining boom began, lawsuits soon were filed in incredible numbers. Between 1880 and 1885 the courts were clogged with cases involving suits for valuable properties, with the majority of the cases coming in 1881-82. Lawyers by the score settled in Tombstone, many of them to earn far more than did the men who struggled in the muck underground for silver ore, even in some cases more than the men who financed the mining and smelting. Many of these lawyers came from California and Nevada, and thus already were familiar with the complexities and intricacies of mining law; others who arrived from the East quickly learned the law, or else to act like they did. Moreover, many of these lawsuits were of such a nature that they required expert underground surveys, so that geologists and engineers also found lucrative employment in Tombstone; the end result of their work was a thorough mapping of the mines of the district, probably better than in any other mining district of the West. Every cross cut, every gallery, every inch of the workings had a map made of them.[14]

Nor were these lawsuits confined only to the major companies. Individual prospectors were just as fond of suing as were the big corporations, while claim-jumping and fraud generated a host of other suits. And individuals would sue each other or the big companies because such suits had sufficient nuisance value that they generally were settled out of court for a far smaller sum than was asked; thus an enterprising man would file a suit with little basis in fact or law, then quietly disappear after being paid a few dollars outside the courtroom. And there were endless lawsuits for non-payment of debts; the Gilded Age Mining Company, for example, was perpetually involved in litigation for everything from failure to pay grocery bills to unsettled boundaries.

Several important or famous lawsuits over mining properties were fought out in the Tombstone courts. Perhaps the most famous case involved the famed "Million Dollar Stope," discovered in 1881; this produced a contest for ownership between the Tough Nut and Goodenough which dragged on for six years before the Tough Nut finally won. Then in 1882 came the suit of the Head Center Mine against the Grand Central. According to the *Epitaph* of January 16, 1882, this legal battle was fought by the largest and most brilliant array of attorneys ever seen in Arizona. Geologists were called to testify, with each side employing its own experts. This case also was memorable for the fact that only eleven jurors made the final determination. There originally had been the usual twelve men, but one of them proved not so true; one morning in the midst of the trial he came into the courtroom so drunk that the judge fined him $100 and sentenced him to two days in jail. The trial proceeded with only eleven jurors with the consent of both parties in the litigation.

The employment of miners, teamsters, workers in the mills, geologists, and even lawyers, along with the merchants who came to sell them supplies, soon brought about the growth of a thriving city. And, naturally, a host of gamblers, saloon keepers, ladies of easy virtue, and even outlaws came to separate the men from their wages and the companies of their bullion. College graduates rubbed elbows with men unable to read and write, and the end result was the growth of not one town but several, the principal of which was Tombstone.

Growth of the Town

Typically in the American West, a mining strike, be it of gold or of silver, acted as a powerful lure to the rootless, restless prospectors and miners who heard of it. Their hopes of participating in the bonanza, of locating rich claims, or of finding employment at high wages, along with their boundless curiosity, drove them to pull up stakes and dash to the new Eldorado. The influx of such large numbers of people naturally brought yet another element hurrying to the spot, those hoping to get rich but without standing waist deep in icy streams panning for gold or working a ten-hour shift mucking in the mines: merchants who wanted to sell goods at inflated prices to these men; lawyers ready to charge exorbitant fees for legal work in connection with settling disputes over conflicting claims; doctors to cure the sick; gamblers catering to the age-old urge to get rich quick; swindlers anxious to ply their wiles on the unwary; "soiled doves" to make money from the paucity of feminine companionship; outlaws ready to rob the fruit of other men's labor. And the clatter of carpenter's hammers notified one and all that cultural institutions—saloons, hotels, and stores, even schools, churches, and jails—were on the way and would be there just as soon as more green lumber and hurdy-gurdy girls could be freighted in. And such was the case at Tombstone and in the vicinity.

One of the first of these towns to spring into existence was near the site chosen by John Vosburg and Dick Gird for the location of the Tombstone Mill and Mining Company's stamp-mill. In the shadow of this structure was an incipient community composed of the employees there; they designated their collection of shacks and hovels "Millville" with the thought that it might develop into a full-fledged town. But such was not to be the case. Across the San Pedro River from the mill, Amos W. Stowe (later a merchant in Tombstone) filed a homestead claim for 160 acres on October 28, 1878; he stated his purpose to be farming and ranching, but on the following February 1 he hired A. J. Mitchell, a civil engineer, surveyor, and assayer, to plat a town site. Early in its existence this town was called Red Dog, but later the name was changed to Charleston after the city in South Carolina; this change was effected by the miners,[1] doubtless those filled with either nostalgia or a sense of humor.

The Charleston townsite company prospered at first as people flocked into the area. Initially the construction mainly was of canvas, but such structures soon were replaced by adobe buildings. By May 1879 the population had grown to 300 to 400, the town had about forty buildings, and twenty-six blocks had been platted, each block with sixteen lots. Five stores, four saloons, an equal number of restaurants, a hotel, two butcher shops, two bakeries, two livery stables, two blacksmith shops, and several service businesses—even one manufacturing plant, a brewery—attended the needs and wants of the town residents. Stowe was able to attract people to his community through the device of offering a three-year lease free to anyone who would live there; inasmuch as these boom towns of the West often did not last three years, the merchants were not taking a big gamble by taking a lot and building, for if the town folded they were not stuck with an expensive but worthless piece of land.

The San Pedro River provided water for the mill and for Chinese farmers who came to irrigate the desert land to grow vegetables. In addition, it supplied the needs of those who would use

Charleston during its boom period. *Courtesy Arizona Historical Society.*

———————————— ∿ ————————————

its water for domestic purposes. At first there was a strong argument about the purity of the San Pedro water; some felt that the river water, as opposed to that secured from wells, would cause fever; time proved that those drinking the river water had fewer problems with fever than did those drinking well water. The San Pedro proved a sufficiently large stream to supply everyone's wants throughout the year—and to exceed the need during the rainy months of July and August when it flooded. For ten months of the year the river could be crossed by fording, but the annual flood during the two summer months led to the construction of a 160-foot bridge in November 1881.

Charleston proved a success. A post office was opened there on April 17, 1879, and even a school was erected to serve the needs of the children brought by family men. The ranchers in the nearby hills traded with the merchants, while Mexicans came north to buy in such numbers that this trade was described as "very extensive" by the Tombstone *Epitaph* on May 6, 1882.

However, Amos Stowe did not profit from this growth and prosperity; on August 14, 1879, he surrendered his holdings because of bankruptcy.[2]

Other small towns with a degree of permanency included Fairbank, which was the site of residence of N. K. Fairbank, organizer of the Grand Central Mining Company. The site received its designation as a town when the El Paso and Southwestern Railroad established a station at the spot in 1882. Fairbank, a Chicago merchant, also was a stockholder in the railroad line that ran from Benson into Mexico, had several other holdings in the Tombstone vicinity, and it was his influence that brought the railroad and the station to the location that received his name.[3] Similarly the town of Contention City grew in the vicinity of another mine, but drew its name from the mill not the developer. At the Contention Mine there was no water, so the mill for it had to be located on the San Pedro (about ten miles northwest of Tombstone). The mill—and thus the town—began operating in 1879, with a post office established there on April 5, 1880.[4] The other city to have slightly more than a fleeting existence was Galeyville, forty-five miles away in the Chiricahua Mountains. It was established by John H. Galey in 1880 at the site of the Texas Mine high in the Chiricahuas; Galey purchased this mine with money he had made in the Pennsylvania oil business, but his town received a bad reputation from the number of rustlers who used it as a headquarters for their activities. The town's location in the mountains made it ideal for their purposes, as did its distance from the seat of law enforcement for that region. The town was abandoned about 1882, however, and never contained more than 300 residents, yet in its heyday it had a post office and a newspaper (the *Galeyville Bulletin*).[5]

But the granddaddy of all the towns of southeastern Arizona which resulted from the silver strike made by the Schieffelins and Dick Gird was that with the same name given the mining district, Tombstone. Originally, however, it seemed that the city would grow in a different location and under a different name. The little store which Gird and Ed Schieffelin opened for the miners at the Tough Nut Mine became the nucleus for this first settlement. Some of the miners employed there threw up shanties, mostly of canvas, because water was to be had there from a wash and from a small running stream. Located in the shade of Tank Hill, named for a tank built on the hill for water storage, this settlement, about three miles north of where Tombstone would grow, was first called Gird Camp but gradually it came to be known as Watervale (or Waterville). But its only air of permanence was the few concrete foundations laid for tents. Yet the site proved unhealthy, and most of its residents agreed that a more propitious location for a city should be found.[6]

Some sources credit John B. Allen, a merchant who had established stores in several mining communities, as the founder of Tombstone, the man who chose the final site for it on a mesa known as Goose Flats.[7] A rival town, Richmond, was established a quarter-mile away by some Virginians, but it quickly faded into insignificance. Then in mid-March 1879, a townsite was purchased by A. P. K. Safford, James S. Clark, and J. H. Palmer; one of the shareholders in this company was Dick Gird, who had been named postmaster for the camp on December 2, 1878. This company employed Solon M. Allis to plot a formal city, which he accomplished in the months following. The streets running in one direction he gave names; those running the other direction bore numbers. And the names he chose for the major streets were easily recognizable: Safford, Frémont (the governor in 1879), Allen, and Tough Nut. Allis had decided that Fremont would be the major thoroughfare, and thus he laid it out eighty feet wide instead of only seventy-five as were all the others. Yet the merchants who built in the town were so independent they disregarded Allis' wishes, and for some inexplicable reason Allen became the equivalent of Main Street, with Fifth and Allen the exact center of the city's business activities.

The deeds which this first township company conveyed to purchasers came under question within a year, for on May 9, 1880, a

Tombstone in 1880 showing the bleakness of its beginnings. *Courtesy Arizona Historical Society.*

Tombstone Townsite Company registered with the territorial land office; according to federal statutes then in force, the deed for this company was registered in the name of the city mayor, by whom it was to be held in trust. At this time the mayor was Alder Randall, and thus he legally became owner of the town lots in Tombstone—apparently the first company formed, the one organized by Safford, Clark, and Palmer, had not gained a legal title to the land on which the town was built. And Randall desired to profit from his unique position, for he sold the townsite in October 1880 to a group of associates who called themselves the Tombstone Townsite Company, headed by none other than James S. Clark.

Suddenly the residents of the city became aware that their deeds were faulty, that they did not own the land on which they had built, that the land legally—if not morally—was owned by a new corporation. Mayor Randall resigned because of the wave of outrage that resulted, while the city council had to content itself with instituting a court suit to void the title of the new townsite company. The Tombstone *Epitaph* of October, November, and December of 1880 is filled with editor John Clum's outrage at his discovery that the Townsite Company was endeavoring to give 2300 Tombstone town lots, out of a total of 2385, to non-resident partners in the company, men living in New Orleans and in California. ". . . Our citizens are to be ousted from their homes, or mercilessly 'bled' by the projectors of said scheme," wrote Clum, "while our city treasury is to be defrauded of the revenue resulting from the sale of lots which must represent in the aggregate over $200,000, a sum which the city can ill afford to illegally and unjustly transfer from its exchequer to the pockets of a scheming few."

Despite such cries of outrage, Randall and the townsite proprietors on November 10 filed a patent for the company at the County Recorder's Office in Tucson, claiming their ownership of the town lots "to have and to hold the same, together with all the rights, privileges, immunities and appurtenances of whatever nature thereunto belonging."[8] Some residents of the town believed the Townsite Company's legal position to be so strong that they purchased their lots a second time; others joined the suit against the company. These cases dragged on for months, some of them resulting in victory for the citizens against the Townsite Company. Judge J. P. Marsh in 1882 declared that "In this controversy between the rightful occupants of the town lots and the speculators, I submit, the law and right is with the former. The mayor in making the deed preferred to make it in violation of a trust and the same should be declared void."[9]

John Carr, who was elected mayor of the city following Randall's resignation, had run on a platform of redeeming the townsite from the promoters, but he apparently did little following his inauguration to right the matter. Soon bitter denunciation of "His Honor" appeared in the "Letters to the Editor" column of the newspapers. And in January 1881, when the regularly scheduled election took place, Carr did not choose to run again. The first Republican candidate, Robert Eccleston, withdrew less than a week before the election, to be replaced by newspaper editor John Clum; he easily defeated his Democratic opponent, Mark P. Shaffer, by a 367-vote margin with slightly fewer than 700 voters going to the polls. Clum stated, "The vital issue was the question of title to the city lots."

While there was a strong dispute over ownership of town lots, a quarrel that would drag on for years and never be fully resolved, the city that grew on Goose Flats did gain legal standing early. Early residents had approached the Pima County board of supervisors, for their town was located within this body's jurisdiction at the time, asking to be incorporated. They stated that incorporation would free Pima County of the expense of preserving the peace in their city inasmuch as incorporation would allow them legally to elect a town marshal; and as a recognized town the residents could enact laws calculated to maintain order. The board of supervisors apparently liked these arguments, for on December 9, 1879, they incorporated the village of Tombstone. There was an effort made at this meeting to change the name of the town, but the board members stated that the name was too well known and left it as it was.[10]

The first house to be erected in the city was constructed in April 1879. Lucius Nutting, a graduate of Rush Medical School in Chicago who arrived in Tombstone in the summer of 1879 to practice medicine, had a dim view of the incipient city: "We found the climate very trying. The camp was new and the town of Tombstone hardly begun—a few shacks and tents but no general store. The town had not been plotted. There was a small muddy creek, and water for domestic purposes was scarce and bad."[11]

By October that year the population had grown to about a hundred residents, but according to another witness the city "didn't look like much." It contained some forty houses, tents, and cabins, with more under construction. Yet one imposing building was up and doing a thriving business, the Cosmopolitan Hotel.[12] And a correspondent for the Tucson *Star* wrote late in 1879 that business in the camp was booming: "The saloon-keepers are always active, polite and accommodating. The restaurants are models of neatness,

Tombstone in 1882. Note that the courthouse had been completed. *Courtesy Arizona Historical Society.*

and supplied bounteously with the choicest meats and such other dainties as the market affords. Mechanics are employed in erecting buildings in various parts of town." And he noted the scarcity of office space, as well as giving a comment about the number of lawsuits under way, when he added, "The lawyers already have more business than they can attend to, simply because they have to carry their offices around in their pockets or hats."[13]

One of the basic necessities of life, water for drinking purposes, was extremely scarce at the site on Goose Flats. To supply this want, enterprising men entered the water business. David S. Chamberlain, for example, dug the first wells and sold his product at $2.00 per barrel. However, competition soon drove the price down to half that amount for a barrel (fifty gallons). One man, driving his own double team to pull a tank wagon with 500-gallon capacity thus could make two trips a day and thereby earn the magnificent sum of twenty dollars for his day's labor. Yet even the price of two cents a gallon led the miners to accuse anyone not bathing in at least fifty cents' worth of water of taking a "spit bath."[14]

Lumber was another commodity in scant supply, and it was desperately needed in the construction of more permanent structures, even those made of adobe. The price was eight dollars per hundred board feet, high by Arizona standards of the day but low for most mining camps in the West. This price forced many of the miners to live in tents, while some of them imitated the Apaches and constructed wickiups of poles and thatched grass. Canvas remained the stable ingredient of building for the first several months—until the sawmill which Gird had sent from San Francisco could supply enough lumber to satisfy the town's needs. Gird's brother and John McCloskey from their location in the Huachuca Mountains made almost as much money from their sawmill as Gird did from his mines. Actually the Dragoon Mountains with their timber were much closer to Tombstone than were the Huachucas, but Victorio and the eastern Apaches, as well as Natchez and the Chiricahuas, made the Huachucas safer to life and limb.

Yet the population listed for Tombstone did not reflect the true number of residents in the area. The town itself might have only a hundred people in it in late 1879, but hundreds more were in the surrounding hills; these were miners and prospectors encamped on their claims. And some of them were sufficiently huddled together for purposes of protection that they gave names to their little settlements, colorful names which reflected the crude frontier humor among the miners; Tombstone could boast of having as suburbs such places as Hog-em, Goug-em, and Stink-em along with the more conventionally named Austin City and Richmond.

These men who flocked to Tombstone almost literally from the ends of the earth did not find transportation too great a problem. Once any mining camp in the West began to boom, some enterprising stage line operator would establish a concern to fill the need. For the city that grew up around the Schieffelins' and Dick Gird's city, the man was J. D. Kinnear. Of shadowy background, Kinnear started his Tucson and Tombstone Express in mid-November 1878, providing once-a-week service between the two cities named in the title of his line. His coach would leave Tucson

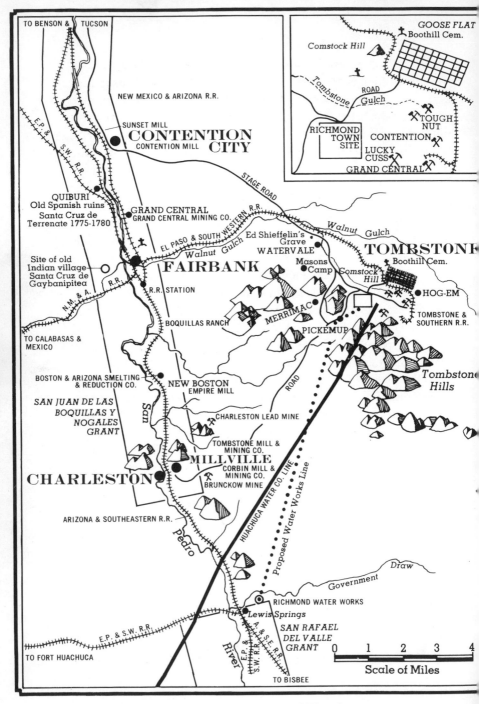

MAP 2 Close Vicinity of Tombstone

on Tuesday, arrive in Tombstone the following day after an overnight stop, and return to the Old Pueblo the following Friday and Saturday. From the first his line prospered although far more passengers rode to Tombstone than made the return trip with him. For the would-be resident of the mining town in southeastern Arizona, once he had reached Tucson (connected with the outside world by regular stage service), the trip began at Rice's Drugstore. There he purchased his ticket from Agent H. C. Walker—ten dollars one way. This steep fare enabled Kinnear, within a few weeks after beginning his service, to purchase with his profits a four-horse Concord coach; this enabled him to cut his road time to only seventeen hours.

The passengers on the Tucson and Tombstone Express were not extremely comfortable, even after the new coach was introduced. Nor was there much in the way of scenery to divert their attention and help while away the monotonous hours. One of them wrote, "There are no towns and few settlers in route, except a little Mormon affair on the San Pedro River [St. David], the way stations of the stages, and three little places between the Contention mill-site and Tombstone, which three places a fellow passenger assured me rejoiced in the popularly bestowed names of 'Hog-em,' 'Goug-em' and 'Stink-em.' "15

Another traveler on this same stage was John Pleasant Gray, a Californian who came to Tombstone in 1880, a graduate of the University of California, Berkeley, who worked in the mines and post office for two years before ranching in the Chiricahua Mountains. He stated, "That day's stage ride will always live in my memory—but not for its beauty spots. Jammed like sardines on the hard seats of an old time leather spring coach—a Concord—leaving Pantano [a stage stop approximately twenty-two miles east of Tucson], creeping much of the way, letting the horses walk, through miles of alkali dust that the wheels rolled up in thick clouds of which we received the full benefit, we couldn't then see much romance in the old stage method of travelling. . . . If it had not been for the long stretches when the horses had to walk, enabling

A Modoc Stage, one used in the early 1880s at Tombstone. *Courtesy Arizona Historical Society.*

---

most of us to get out and 'foot it' as a relaxation, it seems as if we could never have survived the trip."[16]

Kinnear's profits naturally attracted competition, which in turn improved conditions on the run from Tucson to Tombstone. "The Pioneer Tombstone Stage Line" opened under the proprietorship of A. H. Caldwell early in 1880 and began advertising the benefits of "good horses and conveyances," along with a fast trip. And Caldwell cut the fare to seven dollars one way. This effort proved short-lived, but hardly had Caldwell gone out of business when a more formidable rival appeared on the scene: the Ohnesorgen and Walker Stage Company. This operation cut fares between the two towns as well as cut the fees for transporting bullion; it also offered thrice-weekly service each way while simultaneously eliminating the overnight stop; it did this by using six-horse teams, enabling it to advertise "through by daylight—13 hours." Kinnear responded to the competition by offering four trips a week each way and by advertising the scenery of the route he traversed: "This route which is the BEST AND SHORTEST is over a beautifully rolling country and for many miles passes through fine groves of timber, while magnificent mountain scenery relieves the monotony generally accompanying stage travel."

The continued competition soon brought daily service by both companies—and sharply reduced fares: first to five dollars one way, then to four dollars, and finally to just three dollars. At this point both lines were losing money. So they compromised—seven dollars each way became the standard fare, with a charge of three cents a pound for freight. These rates prevailed until rail service sharply reduced their route to just a few miles and then totally out of business in 1902.

Almost from the birth of the town, however, residents had hoped to secure rail service. The Southern Pacific Railroad arrived in Tucson on March 20 to a grand celebration that included cannon salutes and the flowing of great quantities of alcoholic beverages. Fittingly at these festivities, the final spike driven was made of silver taken from the Tough Nut Mine; well that spike might come from Tombstone's mines, for it probably was the ore discoveries in southeastern Arizona that had persuaded Southern Pacific officials to choose a route through southern Arizona rather than follow the Gila River eastward from Yuma across to New Mexico. By June 1880 the Southern Pacific's tracks had reached Benson, after which time the stage lines ran there to pick up people and freight. From Benson it would run on eastward to the New Mexican towns of Lordsburg, Deming, and Las Cruces; then it entered Texas at El Paso and joined the Texas and Pacific at Sierra Blanca.

But even before the Southern Pacific had reached Benson, plans were being laid to get a line into Tombstone. The Arizona and Mexico Railroad and Telegraph Company organized in Tucson on April 3, 1880, projecting its tracks to run from Benson to Charleston, and from there to Tombstone, the tracks to end at Eleventh and Allen streets. A survey was made of this route, and grading began on the right of way in May. W. A. Simmons of Boston, owner of the Empire Mine, was to sell $1,500,000 worth of bonds in the East, but the announcement of a rival which also intended laying tracks from Benson to Tombstone stalled Simmons' progress. The year 1880 ended with all work suspended, no bonds sold, and no railroad in sight.

Then in 1881 came word that Atchison, Topeka and Santa Fe Railroad officials intended to build a line from Guaymas, the Pacific port on the Gulf of California in Sonora, northward to the international boundary and across into Arizona; in fact, construction had begun in May 1880. But the point of entry into the United States for this route was Nogales, far to the southwest of Tombstone in the Santa Cruz River Valley. On June 17, 1881, officials of the Santa Fe filed incorporation papers for the line that would be the American branch of this railroad; called the New Mexico and Arizona Railroad Company, it was to run from Deming, New Mexico, the southern terminus of Santa Fe track, westward to Tombstone and Nogales. However, before construction could begin, Southern Pacific bosses offered the Santa Fe the use of its track between Deming and Benson, whereupon the plans for the N.M. and A. R.R., as the line was abbreviated, were changed to have a spur track running south from Benson to Fairbank and then westward to Nogales by way of the Babacomari River. Again Tombstone was to be left without direct rail connections—and so it was when service began to Contention on March 12, 1882, and trains reached Nogales in October of that same year. There was some talk of a branch from Contention to Tombstone, and grading did get under way in the spring of 1882, but in August it was suspended never to be resumed. Then in 1888 came the formation of the Arizona and South Eastern Railroad Company to build from Fairbank to Bisbee, a burgeoning copper town south of Tombstone, but it also bypassed the silver metropolis. Not until 1902 did this line, now restyled the El Paso and Southwestern Railroad, begin actual grading of the right of way; the track was finally laid on March 25, 1903, and the first shipment directly from Tombstone by rail went out on March 27.[17] By then the city was far past its heyday, and the laying of track produced no revival.

By 1880 the little town served principally by stagecoaches was beginning to be recognizable as a city. Yet it was not without its crudities. George W. Parsons, who arrived in town on February 19, 1880, described it as "one street of shanties some with canvas roofs." Simultaneously he noted that the population supposedly was 2000, most of whom lived outside of town on their claims and coming into town for meals, entertainment, supplies, and excitement. Parsons commented, "Fine broad street. Good restaurants. Good square meal four bits."[18] That year the federal census showed the town contained 973 residents, Charleston had 350, and Contention 150; Fairbank was not listed.[19] Perhaps a better indication of the population of that area can be obtained from the same census, but looking at Pima County (wherein Tombstone was contained); other than the mining district in the San Pedro Valley, Pima County had not grown significantly in population during the decade of the 1870s. Yet the population of the county jumped from 5716 in 1870 to 17,006 in 1880 (despite the fact that part of Pima County had been sliced off and attached to Maricopa County in 1873 and yet another piece had been given to Pinal County in 1877).[20] And by 1881 the estimated population of Tombstone was more than 7000, with a few incredibly optimistic souls even claiming 10,000; this was enough to make it a rival of Tucson for the title of largest city in the territory—and thus enough to make some of its residents aspire for separate county status.

Tucson, as the county seat at which Tombstone residents had to transact business, was irksome to reach. The travel was inconvenient, to say nothing of the expense involved. Yet anyone wishing to record a mining deed or claim or to transact any legal business had to go there. Moreover, most of the county offices were held by people living in the Old Pueblo—and there was no shortage of men in Tombstone who believed themselves capable of exercising a county office. In addition, there were the handsome fees being collected by county officers in connection with the recording of claims, the processing of various kinds of papers, and the serving of writs and other legal documents; estimates of the income of the sheriff of

Pima County at this time, for example, run as high as $30,000—
for which he did virtually nothing except send his deputies out to
do the work. Finally, there was the rivalry between Tombstone and
Tucson for primacy in southern Arizona; as Tombstone approached, and probably surpassed, the Old Pueblo in size, Tucsonians feared the loss of county revenues, a shifting of the Mexican trade, and the loss of primacy in political dominance of the
region to the booming upstart. The *Chicago Daily Tribune* of January 5, 1879, summed up much of Tucson's fears when it stated,
"Tombstone will grow. It is nearer to Sonora than Tucson by
seventy-five miles and is bound to receive a portion of the Sonora
trade which is now worth about $2,000,000 annually."

It was this fear on the part of Tucsonians, plus the desire for
separate county status held by residents of Tombstone, that possibly explains how the people in the San Pedro Valley set about getting what they wanted. W. K. Meade, a member of the council in
the Eleventh Territorial Legislature who called Tombstone home,
announced at the capital in Prescott his intention of introducing a
bill to remove the county seat from Tucson to Tombstone; this bill
was never actually introduced, but it served its purpose. When
Representative H. M. Woods, also from Tombstone, introduced
on January 7, 1881, a bill to create a separate county in southeastern Arizona, one he originally spelled "Cachise" but which was
printed as Cochise, the measure received more favorable attention
than it might otherwise have had. It was referred to the committee
on counties and county boundaries. Four days later H. G. Rollins
of Tombstone introduced a similar measure in the council, and it
also was referred to the committee on county boundaries. And on
January 12, Councilman Rollins presented a petition bearing 1000
signatures to his colleagues, one respectfully asking for the passage
of a measure creating the new county.

Tucson's representatives and councilmen did what they could
behind the scenes to kill the two measures. There even have been
hints that from Tombstone came a "sack," meaning money for
bribes to secure the enactment of the desired legislation.[21] There

were many postponements as the measure came up for a vote, and
when it finally cleared the house it was only to be postponed several times in the council. Simultaneous with this fight, there was
another in the legislature over the location of the capital for the
territory. Originally Prescott had received that honor, but in 1867,
just four years after Arizona had been created a territory, the capital was moved to Tucson; there it stayed for ten years, only to be
returned to Prescott. In 1881 the delegates from the Old Pueblo
were trying to get another vote on the matter. But a measure in the
council that would have returned the territorial capital to Tucson
failed in that house by a vote of seven to five—through an alliance
between delegates from Prescott and Tombstone. And then Prescott's delegates voted for the Cochise County measure, which Governor John Charles Frémont signed on January 31.[22]

Soon afterward another bill designating Tombstone as the
county seat of the new unit of government sailed through with little
opposition. The fight had gone out of Tucson's representatives.
And on February 21 the legislature passed Act No. 39, "An Act to
incorporate the City of Tombstone, to define its limits and rights,
to specify its privileges and powers, and provide for an efficient
government for the same." The measure stipulated that the government would consist of a mayor and four councilmen, one for
each ward and a resident thereof. Sitting together the five men
would constitute the "Common Council" of the city. And the number of councilmen could be increased at the pleasure of the
voters.[23]

Tombstone and its mines dominated the Eleventh Legislature in
other ways than merely securing passage of a bill creating Cochise
County. One of these was repeal of the Bullion Tax Law. Enacted
in 1875 before mining corporations had become a major political
factor, this law did what its title suggested: it taxed the net proceeds of all mining activity on a sliding scale depending upon the
value of the ore extracted. And the rate of taxation, although
minuscule by twentieth-century standards, was sufficiently high to
bother the mining corporations. Both political parties had stated

Tombstone Courthouse which served Cochise County from its completion in 1882 until 1929 when the county seat was moved to Bisbee. *Courtesy Arizona Historical Society.*

their opposition to repeal of the measure, but such a measure slid through easily—again with rumors of a sack of money, reportedly $25,000, being sent from Tombstone to Prescott. And Frémont signed the measure despite the fact that it removed approximately $10,000,000 from the tax rolls of the territory. Even the distant San Francisco *Bulletin* expressed astonishment at the passage of the measure, noting that most of the mine owners receiving these profits were non-residents of Arizona.[24]

But thanks to political maneuvering, Tombstone at last was the seat of government for a separate county, its destiny now in its own hands. The mines were producing a steady stream of profits, talk of railroad connections was in the air, the population was increasing rapidly, and a staccato beat of carpenters' hammers announced the erection of businesses and yet more businesses. This despite the survey of the town then going on and the claims of the townsite company. That first survey of the town in 1881 only increased the bitterness and confusion, for it disclosed that many a man's outhouse or fence, or even his home itself, was on his neighbor's property. For example, the Methodist parsonage was found not to be on church property, and the owner of the land it was on was threatening to hold it for his own use. One evening some of the staunch male members of the church, using large timbers as rollers, moved the parsonage at midnight onto church land.[25]

Of those stores going up in 1879 and thereafter, despite the dispute titles to the town lots, many were colorful. One such establishment was the Golden Eagle Brewery, built in 1879 when the town had only 300 residents. Beer was too bulky and sold too inexpensively to be shipped any great distance before rail transportation was widely available, and thus almost every city of any size, especially those that were mining camps, boasted a brewery. The Golden Eagle Brewery was located in the Wherfritz Building, a two-story structure which also provided office space for Virgil Earp, the deputy United States marshal; his office faced Allen Street. Adjacent to him was Dr. George Goodfellow's office, and next door, some humorously said appropriately, was Dr. H. M. Matthews, who served as coroner. Another person of note who officed in the Wherfritz Building was Wells Spicer, an attorney who would serve as the local justice of the peace in 1881.

When boch beer became extremely popular, the name of the building was changed to the Fredericksburg Lager Beer Depot, and the brewery began serving a good free lunch—provided the patron ate it while drinking beer; and the owners even installed a display of wild animals as an attraction for customers. The lunch they served was very popular, so much so that a frequently heard comment about some resident was that he was "drinking his lunch" at this business. Finally the owners of the establishment decided to add some class to the place by importing crystal stemware and large mirrors, so the name of the business eventually was changed to the Crystal Palace Saloon.[26]

Allen Street, the main thoroughfare of the city, was lined with stores of various types—and numerous saloons. In fact, by 1881 there were 110 liquor licenses in effect in Tombstone. However, liquor was legally sold in many of the stores, so there were not 110 saloons in existence—although it may have seemed that way to a casual visitor. And the gambling saloons did a booming business; there were fourteen faro banks that advertised they never closed, so that a sporting man could risk his money at any hour the fancy struck him. By 1881 these saloons and gambling dens were not of the normal crude, frontier variety; many of them had imported plush furniture, velvet drapes, expensive glassware, and large mirrors, along with bartenders and chefs from St. Louis, New York, and Chicago, bartenders who claimed they could mix any known drink and chefs whose menues backed up their claim that no finer meals could be had from coast to coast.

There were two banks serving the financial needs of this community: a branch of the Safford Hudson Bank of Tucson and a locally owned establishment called the Cochise County Bank. And there were mercantile shops of every variety, many of them advertising that they stocked the latest men's and women's fashions from San Francisco. Hotels included the Cosmopolitan, completed in 1879, and the Grand, built shortly afterward, along with several lesser hostelries.

Completing the picture of metropolitanism by 1881 was the appearance of several newspapers. Almost as common on the frontier as the six-shooter was the printing press; within months, sometimes even within weeks, of the opening of a new town, a printer would arrive with a portable press and a box of type to begin chronicling the events of the new town, usually in the best chamber-of-commerce style. In 1879 the *Nugget* began as a weekly newspaper for the residents of Tombstone, to be followed on May 1, 1880, by a daily and weekly called the Tombstone *Epitaph*. Some sources credit Ed Schieffelin with originating the name of this famous newspaper; he reportedly said that newspapers, like epitaphs, generally did not tell the truth. However, the founding edi-

The office of the Tombstone *Prospector*, a newspaper started in 1887.
Courtesy Arizona Historical Society.

tor of the newspaper, John Philip Clum, later claimed it was he
who coined the title as appropriate to a journal chronicling the
events of a town named Tombstone. Born on September 1, 1851,
on a farm in the Hudson River Valley of New York, Clum had
been desined for the ministry in the Dutch Reformed Church; he
had studied at Claverack Academy and at age nineteen graduated
from Hudson River Institute; then came divinity study at Rutgers
College. But that was interrupted in September 1871 by illness,
and he withdrew to the family farm to recuperate. It was then that
he heard about the organization of weather observations by the
Army Signal Service; he applied for this, was given training, and
then went to Santa Fe, New Mexico, where he worked at the trade
for two years. There in November 1873 he was notified by the Indian Bureau that his church had nominated him for the position
of agent at the San Carlos Apache Reservation. The salary was
$1600 annually—and he accepted it.

Taking command of this reservation on August 8, 1874—just short of his twenty-third birthday—Clum tried hard there to train the Apaches in self-government, organizing an Indian police force, establishing a court at which Apaches presided as judge and jury, and asking that all soldiers be removed from the agency. It was he who removed the Chiricahua Apaches from their old reservation in southeastern Arizona to San Carlos, and it was he who in 1877 went to New Mexico to arrest Geronimo and other renegades and return them to San Carlos. However, he tired of bureaucratic red tape and graft in the Indian service, and he quarreled incessantly with his superiors; moreover, he was disliked by army officers who felt they and not civilians should police the reservations. In disgust with these problems, Clum resigned in August 1877. Moving to Tucson, he wrote, "Tucson, in 1877 . . . midsummer . . . a wife . . . and no job." He had been reading law, so he determined to become a lawyer. A judge in Florence, Arizona, offered him a partnership; this he accepted, and in November of that same year he passed the bar exam. But the law business in Florence was not demanding, and he looked for something to consume his spare time. Thus he became a journalist.

In partnership with some Florence businessmen, Clum purchased the *Arizona Citizen*, then publishing in Tucson, and moved it to his town of residence. This he published as a weekly, soon finding it necessary to drop his law business in order to concentrate on the newspaper. Then, as the Southern Pacific built across Arizona toward Tucson, he anticipated the growth of the Old Pueblo and moved the *Arizona Citizen* back to its original location; beginning in February 1879 he offered it to Tucsonians as a daily. But the rival *Star*, not Clum, was making money from printing contracts and on February 2, 1880, he sold the *Citizen*. Thus he was free to follow the trail of silver to Tombstone where on May 1, 1880, he produced the first issue of the *Epitaph*. By the following January he was mayor of the city—and deeply embroiled in the political, economic, and social quarrels of the area.[27] And these quarrels ran deep—as he would learn.

And, not unexpectedly, Tombstone had a hospital, something desperately needed in a mining town, if not in a frontier area where violence occasionally occurred. There were several doctors of note serving the little community from the first, most famous of whom was Dr. George E. Goodfellow. Born in Downieville, California, on December 23, 1855, Goodfellow was a graduate—with honors—of Cleveland Medical College in 1876. Immediately after graduation he signed with the army as a contract surgeon to serve at Whipple Barracks, Prescott, Arizona Territory. Before his retirement from army service in 1880, he also saw duty at Fort Lowell near Tucson. Thus in the fall of 1880 he arrived at Tombstone; there he would remain for twelve years, publishing in medical journals, returning east periodically to study, and gaining fame as one of the foremost authorities on gunshot wounds in the United States. He was a linguist, a student of philosophy, a dabbler in geology, but in Tombstone he was noted for his sense of humor. While serving as county coroner, he once declared that he had "performed assessment work" on a badly shot corpse and had found it "rich in lead, but too badly punctured to hold whiskey." He was contentious, fighting numerous lawsuits in connection with his business dealings, but a civic-minded citizen who in 1882 fought for a public swimming pool.[28]

The hospital itself was not constructed until 1885. At that time the county board of supervisors contracted to have it built according to plans drafted by Dr. George C. Willis, the county physician. It had a large ward twenty by forty feet with twelve beds and two smaller wards containing two and four beds. The dispensary and operating rooms contained the latest equipment, conveniences, and appliances, with special care devoted to securing the very best surgical instruments. Finally, there was an isolation ward measuring twelve by twenty-four feet separate from the main building, while a third structure contained the post-mortem room. And this structure was pleasingly landscaped with green lawns, shrubbery, and trees.[29]

By the time this hospital was constructed, Tombstone had radi-

John Clum, editor of the Tombstone *Epitaph*. *Courtesy Arizona Historical Society.*

cally changed from its early, crude days—thanks in part to two devastating fires. The first of these occurred on June 22, 1881, and resulted, appropriately, from a barrel of bad whiskey. At the Arcade Saloon, the owner was trying to determine how much of the liquor was still in the barrel, so he would know how much he was returning to the distributor; in the process he dropped the measuring gauge into the barrel. The bartender brought a wire to fish out the gauge—but also brought a lighted cigar with him. There was an explosion, spreading burning alcohol everywhere. The following day the *Epitaph* carried an account which stated that the fire destroyed the saloon and "in less than three minutes . . . had communicated with the adjoining buildings and spread with a velocity equalled only by a burning prairie in a gale." There was no town water supply with which to halt the fire, and it spread until sixty-six stores, saloons, restaurants, and businesses were no more; the total loss was estimated at $175,000, but miraculously no one was killed. And only one man, George Parsons, was seriously injured, he while fighting the conflagration.

When the fire died, the town was rebuilt—one visitor claiming it to be completely reborn within two weeks. More adobes were made and more timber whipsawed out of the Huachucas, and soon the little city was as it had been: combustionable and with no major city water supply. The result was predictable. On May 26, 1882, came yet another fire, this one far more devastating. The flamboyant style of the *Epitaph*, published the following day, captured the event well: "Yesterday morning the bright sun rose over as happy and prosperous a camp as any on the Pacific coast. Ere the God of day sank behind the western hills a scene of desolation and destruction met the eye in every direction. The blackened walls and smoking ruins of what were once handsome and beautiful buildings is all that remains of what was the very heart of Tombstone." This second fire started in a water closet of the Tivoli Saloon, spread rapidly, and burned out the main business section despite the gallant efforts of the volunteer firemen. The

Membership in the three volunteer fire companies of Tombstone carried considerable honor; membership dues were assessed, and fines were levied for non-attendance at meetings. When fires occurred, each of the companies raced to get to the scene first. *Courtesy Arizona Historical Society.*

---

loss in human life was one charred corpse found in the Cosmopolitan Hotel, and in dollars reached perhaps half a million.

This time the city fathers determined on action. Following the fire of 1882 much of the rebuilding was with adobe or brick. And finally a real city water supply was secured. The Sycamore Springs Water Company, which had organized in 1880, had laid a pipe line to bring water from a 500,000-gallon reservoir in the Dragoon Mountains eight miles distant; in Tombstone was a 120,000-gallon tank located on Empire Hill near the city limits. Yet this was not adequate by 1882 for a city claiming 14,000 residents—or even for one which numbered some 10,000 actual citizens. Certainly it was not sufficient to stem the disastrous fire of 1882. Eventually the city would buy this system and use it to supply drinking water only.

A view of the effect of the fire of 1882. A note on this picture states that the men in the picture were guarding their merchandise until the insurance was adjusted. *Courtesy Arizona Historical Society.*

In 1882, following the fire, however, the Huachuca Water Company was organized. Owned by Easterners who reportedly invested $500,000, this company went twenty-one miles away in the Huachuca Mountains where run-off streams were pooled in a reservoir it created to hold 1,000,000 gallons. With seven-inch wrought iron pipe brought from Pittsburg and installed across the twenty-one miles, the company found it could deliver water at the rate of 45,000 gallons an hour in Tombstone with a pressure of 1900 feet at the lowest point. The holding reservoir in Tombstone was cut in solid rock and then cemented; located 365 feet higher than the town with a capacity of 1,200,000 gallons, it delivered water to water mains and fire hydrants at a pressure of 160 pounds to the square inch. This was sufficient to throw a stream of water from a medium-size nozzle to a height of 260 feet—and to knock down an ordinary miner's shack when it caught fire.[30]

Municipal improvements such as a water system heralded the arrival of civilization in its myriad forms. The telegraph came in

1880; by 1883 the telephone provided a connection between corporate offices and the mines, as well as to businessmen and even a few homes. The streets were lighted by gas lamps in 1881, as later would be the homes and stores.

But Tombstone was no quiet, sober New England community. It was boisterous and alive, its streets, a jumble of humanity. Even the newcomer and the stranger would be carried away by the constant hurry of "something doing every minute." Saloons, restaurants, hotels, well-stocked stores, barber shops, gambling halls, all brightly lighted, kept open house on both sides of Allen Street late into the night, and the music from the dance halls and the hubbub of the crowd of men far from the restraints of home and family, young men looking for excitement, filled the air with constant noise. This could be heard miles outside Tombstone and served as an attraction to the lonely prospector and cowboy to come into town and join the gang.

During the day Allen Street seemed only ordinary, like some city thoroughfare in an Eastern setting. But as darkness arrived and the day shift finished its ten-hour stint in the mines, it came to life. People milled about, giving vent to suppressed feelings and good fellowship. They were grown boys out for a night of fun. The nervous man would not have been happy in this setting, for at night he who slept too close to downtown would be awakened suddenly by some unearthly noise, musical or otherwise; by the shout of "Promenade to the Bar" at some dance hall; by the bellowing yell of "Keno" from the throat of a rejoicing gambler; by a pistol shot fired by some "shoot-'em-up Dick" who had read too many dime novels and wanted to hurrah the town. It was like living in a boiler factory—the noise was harmless unless it bothered you, and then it drove you crazy.

And Tombstone was a town of unbounded optimism. Rarely was a hard-luck story heard in the city's streets. Every man expected to strike it rich very soon. As John Pleasant Gray later recalled, "A man might have only a dollar in his pocket, but in his heart he had millions; he could pull from his pockets a number of mining locations, each showing title to 1,500 x 600 feet of untold wealth

Tombstone in 1883 (looking north). *Courtesy Arizona Historical Society.*

needing only development to be another Comstock Lode. He could eat on credit, especially at the Chinese restaurants. Perhaps even trade a location notice for a suit of clothes, especially if the merchant was a newcomer."[31] Life in the city was a living tide of moving humanity, a surging sea of hurrying people, a whirl of excitement, a picturesque and never-ending jumble as the talk swirled endlessly around—always about mines and mining. In the crowded streets men argued over ore samples, prospectors compared location notices and assay certificates, and promoters sought to sell the gullible "the biggest thing in the District."

But all was not work. Each of the 10,000 residents of the city and countryside had moments of relaxation, and each sought it in his own way: some through establishing the refinements of civilization, others by drinking, gambling, and wenching. And all these social pleasantries were available in Tombstone.

Life in Tombstone

It was relatively easy to spot the newcomer to Tombstone and vicinity; the recently arrived gentleman looking to make his fortune had not yet acquired the habit of squinting his eyes. The bright landscape of the desert country, which brilliantly reflected the dazzling sunlight, soon forced men to keep their eyes partially shut—until wrinkles in the pattern of crow's feet were embedded beside their eyes. And the newcomer soon learned that southeastern Arizona's geography forced him into other new patterns of action. During the winter months, the climate was mild compared to the eastern part of the United States, but still was sufficiently cold to make a fire a necessity. In the vicinity of Tombstone, however, a man did not simply fell a tree, chop it into stovewood lengths, and feed it to the flames. Instead his fuel, like the silver he sought, came from the ground. The mesquite was the only tree in the vicinity, and it was the roots that miners burned. "Go out on the treeless valley," wrote John P. Gray, "and look closely on the ground in the neighborhood of a sparse growth of mesquite bushes and you will soon discover long, black-looking roots uncovered in spots. Put your pick under these and pry them up, and it is surprising how soon you can load your wagon with the best stove wood of any land. It is hard wood, but brittle, and will hold the heat like coal."[1]

Another trick the newcomer had to learn was cat stealing if he wanted to get a good night's rest. Heavily infesting the shacks which the miners erected were rats, big ones that foraged at night. As George W. Parsons commented of his first night in Tombstone, "the rats ran about us all night making great racket. Long time before they could be forgotten." Three days later he repeated the same theme in his journal: "Rats and mice made deuce of a racket last night around a fellow's head on ground. Rolled over on one in the night and killed him—mashed him deader than a door nail." The solution to this problem was simple, one followed by most of the miners: steal a cat! The supply was limited, so that the one a miner stole on a given night would be lifted from him in a few days. Parsons learned: less than two weeks after his arrival, he wrote, "Cats are a scarcity and rarity and we sadly needed one. To-night after church we came across two out promenading and Mr. S. and M. B. [his partners] tried to capture one. I was successful and hurried mine home anxious to get there before I was clawed or bitten to death. Peace amongst the rats."[2]

Dogs likewise were prized by the miners, but for a different reason. Those living on the fringes of the Tombstone district feared Apache renegades, and according to local stories the Apaches feared dogs; they barked and alerted the Indians' victims. When the town first began to boom, late in 1878 and through 1879, canines were in such short supply that their theft was prevalent. By 1882, however, there were so many of "man's best friend" in Tombstone that the city council on March 15 passed "An Ordinance to provide for the collection of a license tax on dogs and sluts kept in the City of Tombstone and for impounding and killing of all dogs and sluts upon which the tax has not been paid."[3]

The most widespread diversion for the miners in their off hours was card playing. As Parsons commented soon after his arrival, "Regular routine now nights. Go to town for mail, meat and bread, come home and play cards."[4] But this was not enough for the mass of men living in the hills. Most of them, whether they were independent prospectors or laborers in the mines, were young.

The average life span at that time was far below the Biblical "three score and ten," while the hardships inherent in the work killed all but the physically able or else drove them out of the district. The toil was monotonous and backbreaking; the prospector struggled up dusty arroyos and canyons looking for an outcropping or else did his assaying work on his own claim, while the company employee put in his ten-hour shift below ground mucking and drilling. Both returned at night to primitive shacks for uninviting meals of coffee, beans, and greasy pork. Under such conditions, even in good weather, they suffered from many diseases—diarrhea, dysentery, chills, fevers, and malaria. Men who led such lives could not find sufficient relaxation in playing cards night after night.

Thus they went to town. There some of them drank, gambled, and lied; some frequented houses of ill repute; and some fought, even to the death. But the mass of them hoped and dreamed of a better future for themselves and the city; they planned the families they hoped to raise; they tried to lay away funds for that better day; and they established churches in which they could worship the god of their youth.

In fact, churches were formed in Tombstone almost from the moment of its birth. Parsons, who arrived in the city in February 1880 found services already being held the first Sunday he was in town. In his diary he noted, ". . . I went to church this a.m., hearing one was just started and heard the young minister—McIntyre by name in a tent. Seats of boards resting upon boxes. Good attendance considering." Again on March 14 he wrote, ". . . attended church. Hard wind storm and few present." Two weeks later he noted, "Easter Sunday and good sermon by Rev. Adams of the M[ethodist] E[piscopal] church. He looks after this territory." The quarters for this congregation were temporary; Parsons noted that they were being held "in the theater—a flimsy wooden structure with torn canvas roof." And there were services even on Sunday evenings—the same diarist commented that on Easter Sunday evening there was a "child baptized and communion service. First time for both in Tombstone." But this temporary structure in

which the worship took place was not really suitable, especially
for the minister; as Parsons noted, "Hard work for him to preach
on account of dance house racket in rear. Calls to rally in that
direction do not mingle well—'Hug gals in corner' etc. The place
is rather a poor one for divine service—but best at present I
suppose."[5]

All residents of the city—even those normally shunned by church
people—were well received in the church. Even the "loose women"
of the camp would regularly attend the Episcopal services, then depart for the saloons to resume their usual work at the end of the
worship.[6] And most men of the church-going element thought
nothing of taking a few drinks on Sunday morning before attending church, and then afterward stopping by the saloon for a few
more drinks or even to sit in on a game of chance.[7]

Work on the construction of a church for the Episcopalians pro
ceeded slowly. By August 1880 the walls of a structure had been
erected, but the building could not be completed because of the
rains which, as Parsons noted in his journal, were "hurting adobes.
A great many ruined." Editor John Clum of the *Epitaph*, himself
a member of the church, was moved to editorialize about the slow
progress:

> We presume there is not another town of the same size and age
> of Tombstone in the United States that does not contain at least
> one church. Here, right in the heart of the richest mining country
> on earth stands the unfinished walls of an edifice for church pur-
> poses, that has been in course of operation for months. It can't be
> that Tombstone differs so much from the ordinary mining camps
> in California, where a hat passed to raise money to build a church
> would almost have the bottom knocked out by the contributions
> of all classes of citizens. We don't know who has the matter of
> raising funds for the purpose in charge but we do know that if a
> committee of business men would take the matter in charge, they
> could raise money enough in one day to build and handsomely
> furnish a church. It's a burning shame that the only place of
> worship in town is had through the courtesy of Mr. Ritchie [Clum

here referred to Ritchie's Hall on Fifth Street], himself not a church member, nor particularly religiously inclined.[8]

For a time the Episcopal church was represented in Tombstone by Endicott Peabody, later to gain fame as an educator and founder of Groton Academy. Born in Salem, Massachusetts, in 1857, Peaboy at age twenty-four was attending the Cambridge Theological Seminary near Boston when in 1881 he received a letter from Grafton Abbott, a man who had moved recently from Massachusetts to Tombstone to take charge of a mine; Abbott wrote of the pressing need in the Arizona mining town of an Episcopal minister, calling Tombstone "the rottenest place you ever saw." Peabody then learned that Rt. Rev. George Kelly Dunlop, bishop of Arizona and New Mexico, had visited Tombstone in 1881 to report that the people at that time had raised $1000 for a building and $800 for a minister. This Macedonian call proved irresistible to young Peabody, and he departed for Arizona Territory before completing his studies—and thus before he even was ordained. He began his preaching in the courtroom on Fremont Street and soon had fired the members of his congregation with a zeal to complete the permanent home for the church (ironically, Grafton Abbott, whose letter had persuaded Peabody to move to Tombstone, proved to be a non-churchgoer). Peabody did not remain long in Arizona, however; he returned to Boston in June 1882. Yet his work had been vital: the building was finished, and a regular Episcopal minister was assigned to the parish.[9]

A Catholic priest came from Tucson from the earliest days of Tombstone to celebrate the mass each Sunday. By 1882 construction was under way on a permanent building, one which was dedicated and blessed by the Vicar Apostolic (missionary bishop) of Arizona, John Baptist Salpointe in 1883; he was assisted at the ceremony by the parish priest assigned to Tombstone, Rev. Patrick Gallagher.[10] The Presbyterians and Methodists likewise organized congregations and eventually erected edifices of worship so that by the height of its fame Tombstone boasted four churches.

Interior of St. John's Episcopal Church in 1884, apparently at Christmas. *Courtesy Arizona Historical Society.*

In each of these the women members formed clubs, hosted church suppers and teas, raised money for worthwhile projects, and introduced evidences of civilization.

And there were several fraternal organizations established in the town. Protestants joined the Masonic Lodge, while Catholics had the Knights of Colombus. In addition, the town boasted chapters of the Knights of Pythias, Daughters of Rebecca, the Independent Order of Odd Fellows, and several organizations unknown today—along with such military organizations as the G.A.R. (the Grand Army of the Republic, made up of Union veterans of the Civil War).

Members of the churches joined with members of the fraternal organizations to form their own cemetery. The "nice" people had decided they did not want their loved ones or themselves buried in the same cemetery as the one occupied by deceased gamblers, cutthroats, and prostitutes who were so rapidly filling the only graveyard in town, which was known as "boot hill." They secured a new plot of ground for this purpose. However, some of the fine old families who had already purchased plots in Boot Hill before the organization of the second cemetery continued to use the first one, contributing to a running argument and to social snobbery concerning where good people should have their earthly remains interred.[11]

No such dilemma faced the ladies of easy virtue who flocked to Tombstone to satisfy the lusty needs of the miners. They openly accepted employment as "hostesses" in the many saloons and gambling halls of the city; their job was to greet and entertain one and all who entered the establishment and to get them to purchase drinks. Their pay for this work normally was two and one-half cents per drink, but sometimes it was 20 per cent of what a man spent on liquor. Most of these girls supplemented their income by prostituting. They lived in cheap, drafty shacks clustered behind the saloons, and it was in these that they entertained their male visitors. There was no form of medical inspection available to them —or for the men; in fact, a common rule on the frontier in this regard was that each man looked out for himself, a practice that contributed to rampant venereal disease among both male and female population. These girls, owing to the amount of cheap liquor they consumed, the disease they contracted, the poor housing in which they lived, and the hard lives that they led, died by the score, particularly from pneumonia, which was a major hazard for them.

Yet some of these women were surprisingly honest—and even gentle. Cora Davis was such a lady. She arrived in Tombstone to become one of its most notable madams; she was approximately thirty-five years of age, and of handsome appearance, decorous manner, and good bearing. The house she established boasted girls above the ordinary in appearance, many of them with musical talent. But what set her house apart was her insistence on total honesty in monetary affairs. When a male visitor showed signs of becoming drunk (and all such houses sold liquor as a profitable sideline), he had his valuables taken from him, for which two invoices were made; one was given to him, and the other was kept by the madam. When the gentleman departed at last, his belongings were returned to him—in full.[12]

Another such lady was nameless, at least in the description of her that survives, a dark-haired beauty who occasionally would come to the Crystal Palace Saloon in the afternoons and deal for a gambler known as Napa Nick: "She was a handsome girl—seemed by her manner to have come from a good family. She was always well dressed but nothing flashy, and wore magnificent diamonds."[13] And then there was Madam Moustache and Crazy Horse Lil and Lizette, the Flying Nymph. Some of them advertised their wares in the newspapers under various devices, while others sent out formal invitations such as: "To ———. The pleasure of your company and friends are solicited to attend a Social Party given by me at No. 13 Tough Nut St. On New Years' evening. January 1, 1881. Josephine Harcourt." Others posed for photographs of a pornographic nature; some were stereoscope pictures and their charms could be seen in three dimensions.[14] Residents of Tombstone bragged with civic pride that the local prostitutes were superior in charity, decorum, beauty, manners, even honesty to those of less respectable towns.

And contributing to the number of prostitutes in Tombstone, Charleston, and the other towns of the vicinity were the large numbers of soldiers at nearby Fort Huachuca and other army posts a little farther away. The soldiers of that day were a hard lot; some were Civil War veterans unable to settle into tame civilian pursuits after that conflict had ended; some were toughs from the cities who had been encouraged to leave town by local judges and police; some were hard immigrants recently arrived from Europe; and others were simply young lads in search of adventure. Moreover, army life made them even harder, for soldiering in this period was not easy. Thus when they received their monthly pay, they went to the nearest town looking for whiskey and women. James Wolf later commented, "that old soldier whisky was awful stuff, ditto the women." Somehow the prostitutes of Tucson and even cities to the north always knew when the paymaster would arrive at each army post, and the girls would begin arriving at Tombstone just before he did with the money. Once paid, the soldiers were given passes, and they swarmed into town. What money they did not waste on whiskey and women was lost at the gambling tables. And should the soldier somehow manage to withhold a few dollars from those three snares, the women would steal them when he was drunk. Those soldiers who first went broke would be, of necessity, the first to sober up and return to the fort; when enough men had returned, the officers would organize them into a squad of military police, march them to Tombstone, and round up the rest to be herded back to the military installation.[15]

The few decent, single women in town were widely courted. When a new school teacher arrived or when a family with one or more marriageable daughters moved into town, many an otherwise tough miner began to think of taking a bath and securing a better suit of clothes. The stricken male would spruce up his appearance —he would slick down his hair with soap, trim his beard—and he would go to church to secure an introduction to the lady of his choice. If given the encouragement of ever so fleeting a smile from the damsel, he would then invest in a suit of store clothes. And if the swain felt himself a fair hand with Mr. Colt's pistol, he might even purchase a derby hat, which to wear on Allen Street was to court a fight; someone would knock off such head-covering, and first one and then another would kick it along, soon making it not worth recovering. If the owner was a dude and took the incident good naturedly, the crowd usually would chip in to purchase him the regulation soft (cowboy) hat. If, however, he was an old hand who should have known better, then he had to be prepared to fight to defend his choice of headgear.

With this new finery, the young man, sweating in a stiff collar "like a government mule" and with everyone of his corns aching, then would attend the local church bazaars to be separated from his money by pressure to purchase raffle tickets. One observer of this, the effect of love, summarized such antics by stating that it all was done "for the sake of a new face and the opportunity to learn to curl their little finger around a tea cup in the toniest fin-de-siècle manner of the day, when straight whisky and the Bird Cage was really their calibre."[16]

One ready source of brides for the miners, as well as the cowboys in the vicinity, was the public school system. As in so many frontier towns of the American West, the first parents to arrive wanted a good school system for their children and would proceed to organize one. Under Arizona law passed in 1871, at the urging of Governor A. P. K. Safford, every town was entitled to form a school district with the right of local taxation, and such districts would receive additional funding from the territorial treasury. Tombstone saw its first school opened in February 1880 in a small room with a dirt floor. There were nine pupils. Before the end of that first term, the number of students in attendance had grown to more than forty. The desks were crude, consisting of boards resting on packing boxes; seats were made by placing planks on nail kegs; and the teacher's desk was a flour barrel turned upside down. Textbooks were of every variety—any book that was found was used.

In Charleston the school building was a small unpainted house, its sides covered with morning glories and surrounded by mesquite trees. In it the students sat four on a bench, each with a home-made desk in front of him, with the smallest children in the front, the biggest students in the back. The first teacher was a male, H. E. Witherspoon; he was followed the next year by Miss Ella Foy. One student at that school later recalled, "There were not many pupils when I first entered school—perhaps a dozen. . . . We had a man teacher, the first year. . . . the next teacher, Miss Foy . . . knew the subjects where the man didn't. . . ."[17]

Teaching school under such frontier conditions could be very trying. Many of the teenage boys thought of themselves as men in-asmuch as they did a man's work when not in school. In Tomb-stone some of them even went to school packing a pistol. One Tombstone teacher solved this problem by taking all the boys' guns and throwing them into the stove—but she forgot or did not know first to remove the bullets. There was resulting excitement. In Charleston, the first teacher, Mr. Witherspoon, instituted a system of checking student weapons at the door as men were required by law to do as they entered the town saloons.[18]

Gradually the school system in Tombstone improved as funds became more available and more students enrolled. And for adults there were night courses in penmanship and language. Before the end of the decade of the 1880s, the schoolhouse was a two-story edifice with modern appliances. The children were divided into grades with separate female teachers for each of the primary grades. A visitor to the city in 1889 wrote, "During a residence of three or four weeks in this city, we have rarely heard a coarse or vulgar word proceeding from a youthful mouth, and we feel inclined on that account to give credit alike to teacher and parent. . . ." Thus under frontier conditions, with crudity and profanity on the part of drunken prospectors and cowboys ever before the young, the school system performed remarkably well. Discipline was very strict. As the visitor in 1889 remarked, Tombstone's young people would "compare favorably in demeanor and intelligence with a like number anywhere in the land."[19]

The Tombstone City Band, 1883. Volunteer musical organizations were numerous in the city during the bonanza years. *Courtesy Arizona Historical Society.*

There also were other evidences of literacy in the town. The Tombstone Club was formed by citizens interested in securing the latest magazines. By pooling their resources they were able to subscribe to some sixty periodicals. Rental libraries made a point of securing copies of new books published both in the United States and England. Literary societies occupied the evenings of many young men, while volunteer bands were formed by miners who had both a knowledge of music and an instrument; these organizations gave free concerts and played at the numerous dances which were organized. Moreover, there were free speeches on diverse subjects given by experts and amateurs which anyone with an interest could attend. For example, Dr. Goodfellow, in addition to practicing medicine, was an avid student of geology, and thus he rushed to Bavispe, Sonora, on May 31, 1887, to investigate a particularly severe earthquake; then on February 8, 1888, he delivered an address at the school "to a large and cultured audience. . . . The lecture was illustrated by charts and diagrams, and was from the novelty of the subject a particularly interesting one."[20]

Another free pastime and amusement was gossipping. Tombstone was a boisterous and uninhibited town, one where numerous pranks were played and one with a rich diversity of individualists about whom the residents could speculate. For example, there was Russian Bill, reportedly a former lieutenant in the Imperial White Hussars of the tzar; wanting to see the American West, he applied for a leave in 1880, received it, and came to Tombstone. There he dressed like an outlaw, and he associated with the lawless element. However, he joined with Sandy King, a local thief, in a foray to steal horses in New Mexico; there at the little town of Shakespeare they were caught—and hanged by vigilantes without the formality of a trial.[21]

There were endless subjects for discussion in Tombstone, such as the duel fought by Patrick Hamilton and Sam Purdy on September 18, 1882. Hamilton was editor of the *Independent*, while Purdy was editor of the *Epitaph* between May 1 and July 29 that year; the two castigated one another in print until Purdy demanded satisfaction on the field of honor. Inasmuch as dueling was illegal in Arizona, they met just across the international line in Sonora. At 10 a.m. the two antagonists, with their seconds and physicians watching, stood facing one another ten paces apart. Hamilton as the challenged party claimed the right to furnish the weapons, and he produced two Colt .45 revolvers purchased the day before in Tombstone. Purdy refused to use the pistol selected for him, however, saying his arm was too weak for the heavy weapon and that he could not cock it. He thereupon produced two dueling pistols, but Hamilton refused to use one of them on the grounds that they had been in Purdy's possession for some time and that he had practiced with them, thereby gaining an unfavorable advantage. This impasse over weapons ended the "duel," and the two men withdrew from the field of battle—to be greeted by hoots of merriment from residents of Tombstone.[22]

But the major entertainment for young Tombstone was the theater. As early as March 1879 a traveling group appeared in a make-shift structure in the city; "Billy Brewster's Minstrels have been out to Tombstone on a trip and are back again," declared the Tucson *Arizona Star* on March 31, 1879. This first group was followed in rapid order by the English Opera Company, which performed "Pinafore on Wheels" during the first week in December of 1879 to capacity audiences. Attorney Wells Spicer commented about cultural growth in Tombstone in a letter which appeared in the Tucson *Star* of February 29, 1880: "The town is not altogether lost, even if there is a population of 1,500 people, with two dance houses, a dozen gambling places, over twenty saloons and more than five hundred gamblers. Still, there is hope, for I know of two bibles in town. . . ."

By the summer of 1880 several theaters had been erected. Danner & Owens Hall, on Allen Street, had a large auditorium boasting chandeliers and theater boxes along with curtains and foot-lights. The Sixth Street Opera House had been completed some-time early in 1880; later known as the E. Fontana Dance Hall, it also was called the Free and Easy. And there was Ritchie's Hall on Fifth Street which was used for dances and union meetings, as well as by traveling theater troups. And Turn-Verein Hall, located on the corner of Fourth and Fremont streets, had similar usage.

But the best known and most imposing of all the theaters was Schieffelin Hall, for two decades the largest and best-known theater between El Paso and San Francisco. Construction on this edifice, the brainchild of Ed Schieffelin, began early in 1881 and was complete by May of that year. The largest adobe building in the United States, it stood two stories high and 130 feet long, with a seating capacity of 700 and a ceiling 24 feet high. In addition to its 40-foot-wide stage and its auditorium, it also provided housing for the King Solomon Lodge of Free and Accepted Masons. Into it were booked legitimate plays, operas, musicals, and lectures. The Tucson *Arizona Star*, in describing it in an issue on March 16, 1881, declared, "From top to bottom it is by far the most complete

Schieffelin Hall before its recent restoration. *Courtesy Arizona Historical Society.*

edifice of the kind in the Territory. The drop curtain is a Colorado scene and is a work of art."

Schieffelin Hall was the site for legitimate theater, but it was the Bird Cage that the miners gravitated toward. The Bird Cage was the handiwork of William J. Hutchinson, himself a former variety performer who had arrived in the city early in its history to purchase the town lot on which he would build for only $600. It offered itself to the public on December 23, 1881, and became a sensation; men flocked to see its resident variety troup—and three bartenders—perform. The girls who danced in the skits, providing hilarity for cowboys, cattle rustlers, smugglers, miners, and the few staid pioneers who visited it, also worked as barmaids—and more—to supplement their income. The entertainment was not highbrow; it consisted of leg shows and bawdy blackouts along with the normal variety acts. An anonymous "Special Correspondent" for the Tucson *Star* sent a report printed on October 19, 1882, that indicated the work performed by the "actresses":

> After depositing two bits with the door-keeper, I entered a hall filled with old age, middle age, bald-head age (next to stage), youthful age, and boy age—all sitting around tables drinking pro-

miscuously with the "cats." I seated myself at one of them and was surveying the gallery when a dizzy dame came along and seated herself alongside of me and playfully threw her arms around my neck and coaxingly desired me to "set 'em up." All knowing my bashful and guileless ways can imagine my "set back." I thought that all the congregated audience had their eyes on me, and the hot blood surged through my cheeks. Her bosom was so painfully close to my cheeks that I believed I had again returned to my infantile period. To escape from this predicament I immediately ordered them up. She and I, after drinking the liquid, parted at last—she in search of some other gullible "gummie."

About two in the morning, when the girls in the show became tired of performing and then going down into the audience to hustle drinks, the chairs and tables would be stacked back and everyone danced—and drank—until dawn.

Among the favorite performers who played the Bird Cage was Pearl Ardine, whose specialty was jig-dancing and who, according to newspaper reports, could "pick up money thrown her and place the same in her stocking without losing a step." Another was one Mrs. De Granville, who was billed as "the woman with the iron jaw"; she performed a strong-woman act that packed the Bird Cage during her stay. And Nola Forrest, a comedienne, played the house in 1883, leaving behind a bookkeeper, J. P. Wells, to be arrested for embezzling more than $800 from the Boston Mill Company to buy her jewels.

Almost anything seemed possible at the Bird Cage. In June 1882 the ever-popular stage version of *Uncle Tom's Cabin* was being performed. Just as Eliza crossed the icy river, a drunken cowboy in the audience, feeling sympathetic to her plight, shot the bloodhound that was pursuing her; fortunately it was a real dog and not a human, but the audience was nonetheless so incensed that the cowhand was severely beaten before he could be rescued and thrown into jail by the sheriff. The next day the sobered and sorry cowboy shed tears over the dead dog and offered his money and his horse as recompense.[23]

Interior of the Bird Cage Theater, from a painting. *Courtesy Arizona Historical Society.*

And showman Hutchinson—Billy he was called—always had a ready surprise to keep the Bird Cage audience happy. One evening a noisy, apparently drunken customer in one of the boxes kept shouting invective and catcalls at the performers. Hutchinson came on stage to ask that the man calm down, but the request seemed only to infuriate the shouter. With a great show of reluctance Hutchinson sent the bouncers to eject the noisy patron. Their arrival at the man's box was followed by shouts, then the noise of a fight, and finally by a pistol shot. Horrified spectators looked up to see a man's body thrown from the box onto the stage—only to realize suddenly that the "body" was a dummy made of straw! The whole incident was a hoax.

Because of the number of theatrical productions being staged, the city fathers decided to raise revenue therefrom. Ordinance No. 58, adopted on April 5, 1881, stated, "For every show or theatrical exhibition and all kinds of public amusement, a daily license of five dollars . . ." was to be paid. This tax doubtless produced considerable revenue, for to Tombstone in its few years of glory came some of the most famous theatrical troups of that day. Nellie Boyd was among the first, bringing her "Dramatic Company" to town on November 29, 1880, for a three-week engagement at Ritchie's Hall. A native of Chicago with experience in New York, Miss Boyd opened with *Fanchon the Cricket*, followed by several other plays (pirated for her repertoire in that pre-copyright day). And she apparently was impressive; diarist George Parsons, who was familiar with theatricals in San Francisco, termed her efforts "very good." Her opening-night success was repeated every night of her stay—all to a full house, "standing room being at a premium and many being turned away from the door."[24] Not surprisingly Miss Boyd visited Tombstone several more times in the next three years; she stopped only when the mines—and with them the audiences—began to decline.

Other notables to play Tombstone included Eddie Foy, who was at the Bird Cage and who commented that the theater should have been named the Coffin, for it was built in the shape of one. And there was Robert McWade, who graced the Sixth Street Opera House in April 1881; for this engagement the stove, bar, and other encumbrances were removed to make room for 150 seats as he enacted *Paddy Miles' Boy* and his ever-popular *Rip Van Winkle*. Tombstone also was visited by a number of touring "professors" (that is, magicians, ventriloquists, slight-of-hand artists, and even lecturers); for example, E. C. Taylor came not only to play the Turn-Verein successfully but also to perform a benefit for Tombstone Engine Company No. 1. Lesser professors who graced the Tombstone stage included E. C. Willson and Marc Cristol, who were professional wrestlers of the Graeco-Roman style. Yet another form of entertainment popular in that day was the minstrel show, and Tombstone saw such notables as Callender's Minstrels, M. B. Leavitt's Minstrels, and the Great Western Minstrel Troupe.

Understandably some of these visiting thespians caught silver fever—to their regret. James O'Neill, a romantic lead (the father of playwright Eugene O'Neill), proved an easy mark in 1880 when he fell into the clutches of a swindler named George M. Ciprico. Himself a sometime amateur actor, Ciprico in 1879 salted a claim in Tombstone known as the Cumberland Mine; then, as was the custom, he issued a handsome prospectus offering shares for sale. John E. Owens, an actor with little knowledge of mining, visited the site, failed to detect the swindle, invested in the property, and then persuaded O'Neill and a third actor, Louis Morrison, to buy shares. They invested to the point of ownership, only later to file for bankruptcy after losing their savings. Local wits later dubbed the site "The Actors' Mine."[25]

Despite the number of touring companies to play Tombstone— or perhaps because of them—several local citizens were encouraged to try their hands at amateur productions. Among those who thirsted to tread the boards were John P. Clum, newspaper editor and mayor of the city, and George W. Parsons, miner, real estate dealer, and diarist. On February 23, 1880, the Tucson *Arizona Star* noted the start of amateur theatricals in Tombstone by stating, "Shakespeare's ghost is prowling about this argentiferous graveyard. They have organized a dramatic association here." The first amateur group to offer itself to the public was the Tombstone Glee Club; the *Epitaph* reviewed their initial effort at the Oriental Saloon on July 29, 1880, with little effort at understatement: "They are immense!" Then on October 1 that year a benefit was staged at the Presbyterian Church by the amateurs; featured that evening was Mayor John Clum reciting "The Spirit of Wine" and then joining a quartet to sing "Away to the Fields." The highlight of the evening was an original song, the words of which were written by Ed Schieffelin, entitled "Tombstone Camp." The first theatrical production by amateurs in Tombstone was offered on November

6, 1880, a musical comedy called *Andy Blake, or The Irish Diamond;* the play was followed by a concert and grand ball, the proceeds from which went to the Catholic Church and the town hospital.

The town fire of June 22, 1881, gave impetus to the local amateur actors. Following this disaster they formed the Tombstone Dramatic Relief Association and staged a melodrama, *The Ticket-of-Leave Man,* in Schieffelin Hall for one-dollar admission; it raised more than $400 and was repeated two nights later, the money used to purchase a fire alarm bell. Then on October 18 the amateurs staged a "Musical and Literary Entertainment" at the Mining Exchange Hall, which also proved a "literary and financial success." Not all the amateur productions were of such high artistic content, however; for example, on February 9, 1884, Parsons noted in his diary, "Lots of fun tonight. Wrestling match to a fine house. Milton M. and I on stage. Ed Willson's second, Gates, the San Pedro wrestler, selected me to keep time, but Maurice had a stop-watch and I deferred to him. Exciting."

Thus in Tombstone the miners had a wide assortment of organized entertainment available to them: plays, both amateur and professional, teas, benefits, concerts, and dances. Again it was George Parsons who summed up the activities of the town: on the same day that Bisbee bandit John Heath was lynched in the morning, a Washington's Birthday social was held; Parsons commented in his journal, "Hanging in A.M. and Dance in P.M. Good combination."[26]

On an ordinary evening, however, the miners gravitated toward the saloons for a few drinks. Most of these saloons did not hire theatrical troops to lure imbibers into their establishments; they merely sold their whiskey and beer a little cheaper than did the more pretentious "theaters," and they tried to make money from gambling. Every saloon, whatever its pretensions, was certain to have as part of its regular equipment one or more roulette wheels, along with faro and poker tables. Most of them were open twenty-four hours a day, seven days a week, and they were designed to

The Oriental Saloon where the Earps dealt faro. *Courtesy Arizona Historical Society.*

separate the cowboys and soldiers from their pay, the prospectors from their dust, and the transients from their savings—for the enrichment of the saloonkeeper, his stable of girls, and the horde of professional gamblers who haunted the town. A few of these saloons made a pretense of respectability, but all were run with a flexible code of ethics—i.e. the games were as crooked as the owners could make them and still attract business. Many of the gamblers had come to Arizona as refugees from vigilante justice in Nevada, Montana, or elsewhere; a few of them were from far-off Australia, while others had come from the East and the urging of the police. If these gamblers could win by luck or clever play, that was fine; but if they found it necessary to use marked cards on a tenderfoot or a greenhorn, that also was fine.

And if the gambler decided he had to ignite gunpowder, he did so with the intention of killing. A man only wounded might shoot back—or even live to take the witness stand at a trial and testify against the man who shot him. For this reason most gamblers usually went well armed. A .45 might be in open evidence, but it rarely was used. Rather these men preferred what was called a "house gun" or "hideout gun" or "pepper-box"—a small-calibre, multiple-shot, easily fired weapon kept under the table or concealed on the person. The regular miners, freighters, prospectors, and soldiers were good fighters and rarely would take back-talk from anyone, but when it came to facing one of the gamblers the non-professional usually did not argue.[27] Bad as they were, however, Tombstone's saloons were considered high class in comparison to those of Charleston.

The diverse origins of the gamblers can be seen in John P. Gray's description of a well-known resident of Tombstone, a man known locally as Napa Nick: "A professional gambler of the old school, he looked more like a sedate judge. He was often called 'Judge' by many. He was white-haired, wore Uncle Sam chin whiskers and was always dressed in a sedate black suit." One day two men came to town and asked to see Judge Nicholls of Napa City, California. Directed to Napa Nick, they recognized their man but were much taken aback to learn he was a gambler. Later they told witnesses that the Nicholls' residence at Napa City was one of the show places of the town and that the judge's wife and two pretty daughters moved in the best social circles. They concluded by stating that, although the judge was away most of the time, he was a liberal contributor to many charities, a leading benefactor of the town, and one of its most admired citizens.[28]

Another rough source of amusement in Tombstone, one imported from Mexico, was cock fighting. The roosters used in these bouts were brought north from Sonora and even from faraway Chihuahua, and generally they were handled by their Mexican trainers. Hundreds of dollars might change hands during a single match as men put money on their favorites. A roped-off enclosure in some vacant lot provided the only setting needed. A master of the fight would be chosen to act in the capacity of referee, announce the names of the contestants and give their point of origin along with

A cock fight in Tombstone, 1882. *Courtesy Arizona Historical Society.*

past records, and start the fight. The "setter-to," who acted as manager for each cock, would bring his rooster into the pit, and the rules would be announced. These preliminaries out of the way, each setter-to would take a mouthful of water and blow a fine spray under the wings of his bird. Then each would place his bird on the ground, hand covering the beak and pointing it toward his opponent. Then at the signal of the master of the fight, the men released the roosters and stepped out of the ring. Generally the birds could not be touched by the setters-to after they were released; to do so was to concede defeat. If a bird refused the challenge, he again would be placed breast-to-breast with his opponent in the pit's center; if a second time he refused to fight, he was considered defeated.

Rarely would these imported fighting cocks refuse to fight, however. Once released in the pit, they would shake themselves, ruffle their plumage, and then advance on each other, their heads high, their neck feathers ruffled, prancing around in little jumps, their eyes glittering. Then would come vicious jumps, breasts would thump together, and finally one would leap into the air with a spur flashing—bringing blood. Sometimes the fight would be over with one single lucky slash that hit a vital point; usually, however, the birds would separate to circle and jump and slash for several moments before a gradual loss of blood brought one of the birds to its deathbed. This miniature "moment of truth" would bring shouts of delight from those winning bets and groans from the losers—along with calls for a pair of fresh birds to be produced.

And naturally in a society where horses were a vital means of transportation, arguments about the relative merits of the various animals could be settled in only one way, by racing, just as bragging about a special horse invariably would produce a challenge. On these impromptu races hundreds of dollars likewise would change hands. Even the Indians would join in these horse races, as James G. Wolf reminisced: "Sometimes a bunch of Papago Indians and their families would come down from Tucson with ponies they wanted to race, trade or sell. Then we might have several days of horse racing, but as fast as the Indians sold anything for cash, some bootleggers would sell them whiskey and it always ended with the Indians going home afoot across country empty handed."[29]

There were few athletic team sports which the miners could participate in because baseball and football had not yet become national pastimes. However, a man could hunt and fish endlessly if he cared to risk the Indian menace. The San Pedro was a live river filled with fish, especially behind the many dams built to hold water for the mills and for irrigation. And the Huachuca and Dragoon mountains teemed with deer and quail—and even bear if the hunter was sufficiently adventurous. No hunting or fishing licenses or other impediments then existed, and the territory had no gaming seasons, so that a man could decide at a moment's notice to hunt or fish either for meat or for entertainment.

Finally in Tombstone there was the unexpected. For example, one evening there appeared on Allen Street a man dressed like a Gypsy and wearing big, hooped earrings—and leading a cinnamon-colored bear by a short chain. Such an unusual sight naturally brought a large crowd in short order, so large in fact that virtually all business activity in town ceased. To the great delight of the crowd the Gypsy proved no casual tourist, for he announced to them, when he secured quiet, that his was a wrestling bear. He said he was willing to bet five dollars with any individual wanting to wrestle his beast, the winner to be the first to lay the other down in the street. The miners looked at the bear, which appeared small as it stood on all four feet, and a line of challengers quickly formed.

Just as the first match was to take place, however, the bear stood on its back feet—and was at least a foot taller than the tallest man present. One witness to this event declared, "No man's arms were long enough to encircle his cinnamon-colored highness around the middle."[30] Yet the miners were still willing to wrestle the beast, for the concensus was that victory could easily be had: all a man had to do was pick up one of the bear's feet and throw him off balance, thereby winning the bet. "But," wrote the witness, "the monster stood like a statue, and no one was even able to lift the bear's leg even the least little bit from the ground."

Despite the shouting, laughing, and excitement, the bear stood patiently. He seemed confident of his power, simply standing and waiting as each contestant in his turn pulled and tugged and pushed and groaned and shoved; then, at a single word of command from his owner, "Mr. Bear would place his paws around his opponent's body, gently lift the man off the ground and as gently lay him down in the dust of the street." Defeat after defeat for the humans did not deter more challengers; almost every man in the crowd wanted a turn "and the five dollar bills fell on the Gypsy like rain." Murmurs ran through the crowd that bear wrestling was more fun than anything that had ever occurred in Tombstone.

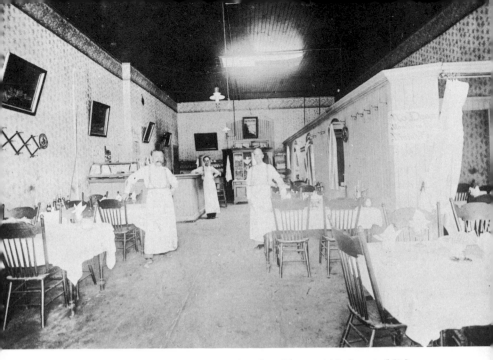

Interior of the Can Can Restaurant. Local residents said the establishment was appropriately named inasmuch as everything it served came from cans. *Courtesy Arizona Historical Society.*

Darkness finally forced a halt to the wrestling, but the crowd was not satisfied; in loud voices the miners urged the Gypsy to return the following day so that the contest could be continued, and he agreed at last to do so. But the next day he was gone, never to be seen again—whereupon rumor spread, probably with good reason, that the owners of the saloons, dance halls, and gambling dens had collected from among themselves a heavy purse which they gave the Gypsy as an inducement to leave town with his bear. His presence had caused their businesses to suffer heavily.

Thus Tombstone in its heyday had virtually everything a young man might want—with the possible exception of enough nice young ladies to court. Yet it was the absence of wives, sweethearts, and mothers which enabled them to lead the carefree, wild life of bachelors. Their wages were high in comparison to those received by workers in the East; miners made twenty-four dollars a week, while teamsters received forty to sixty dollars a month and board, clerks got from fifty to one hundred dollars a month and board, and day laborers were making two and one-half to three dollars a day. Board could be had in town for eight to ten dollars a week, and rent cost approximately twenty dollars a month. In the restaurants the evening meal was fifty cents, with breakfast and lunch costing less. The miner who cooked his own meals found that sugar and coffee cost twenty cents a pound, bacon twelve and one-half cents a pound, potatoes two to five cents a pound depending on the season, and flour went for five dollars per hundred pounds. These unrestrained, ebulient young men thus led a life alternating between hard, dirty work and a frantic search for fun and relaxation. Some later would recall the life as pleasant, while others would comment simply that "Tombstone sure was a bad town. I didn't stay very long. . . ."[31]

Helping convince some of those men that life in Tombstone was bad was the feuding—and fighting—between the faction vying for riches without work and that struggling to impose order and justice. Tombstone's search for stability and maturity would include such bloody antics as robberies, murders, and open shoot-outs in its streets, but the men who participated in these incidents defied easy labeling as "good" and "bad." Sometimes they were both—simultaneously.

Good Guys and Bad

Myth and legend have grown about Tombstone's law-bringers and law-breakers until, like ivy on a house, the true outline of the city's past has been obscured. No word in the English language so evokes an image of two men stepping out into the middle of a dun-baked, dusty, deserted street to face one another in mortal face-to-face, pistol-to-pistol combat as does Tombstone. The armor of the good man is buckskin, his lance and sword a Colt. 45, his battle that of righteousness versus evil; the villian is sustained by the knowledge of his own proficiency with weapons and his total disregard for human life. Yet these pasteboard characters, who form part of a unique American morality play, never lived in actuality, although they have enlivened so many Saturday afternoon matinees and so many nights in front of the television screen. They did not inhabit Tombstone, or for that matter anywhere else in the American West. They were deliberately invented. Yet the passions that have been generated by pulp and celluloid are of such strength and are so enduring that to write of them is to stir up historical controversy, inflame reason, and court condemnation.

The city that grew on Goose Flats did have its share of law-bringers and law-breakers, as has every Western boom town. Precious metals in sufficient quantity always attracted men who would profit without working, while those who toiled would band together to elect peace officers for the purpose of protecting life and property. The West of the 1870s and 1880s was new and raw and in the process of development, without the restraints and refinements of the more effete East; to the West drifted men with cloudy pasts, some to rectify past mistakes and others to repeat them. Tombstone was no exception, and thus whether a man was organizing a gang or a posse he always could find followers.

To suggest that Tombstone was evenly divided between good men and bad, that the balance was nearly equal, is incorrect. The majority of the men toiled sixty hours a week in the mines or mills and thus did not have time for endless drinking and gambling; they did not sit in bars waiting for gunfights so they could act as witnesses to the violence. Most of the men were law-abiding, if somewhat prankish in their sense of humor and even given to fits of uncontrollable behavior. These were men far from home; they worked hard without the comfort of family and loved ones; and they drank too much bad liquor. But the element that would rob and kill constituted only a miniscule portion of the population—yet it has been this portion that has been most remembered, most chronicled, most celebrated.

From the moment of its birth, the Tombstone mining district and the cities in the vicinity had a legal structure and legal authorities. Inasmuch as it was in the United States, it was subject to federal statutes—as represented by a United States marshal who resided in the territory and who could appoint deputies, and by United States judges in their federal district courts; because it was located in Arizona Territory, it was subject to the normal territorial officials and courts; and as part of Pima County it answered to the sheriff, his deputies, and the county and justice of the peace courts. Moreover, Tombstone had an additional legal layer, the local one, first authorized by its incorporation as a village on December 9, 1879, by the Pima County board of supervisors. This allowed the appointment of a town marshal and the establishment of a justice of the peace court, along with passage of village ordinances.

The mayor and city council quickly moved to establish "peace, good order, health and safety . . . and for the protection of property" by means of Village Ordinance No. 3. This set a maximum fine of $100 and/or one month in the village jail for drunkenness, disorderly conduct, sleeping in the streets or on sidewalks, using profane language, making indecent gestures, discharging a firearm except in a duly licensed shooting gallery, racing a horse in the streets faster than six miles an hour, keeping hogs within the village limits, and slaughtering animals in town.[1]

Moreover, there were periodic moves in Tombstone to outlaw the wearing of guns in public. And customarily a man left his firearms at the livery stable or with the bartender at the first bar he entered. There were then, as now, people who objected to being stripped of their firearms. Yet what most irked the residents of the town was the practice of gamblers and swindlers of carrying concealed weapons, so that the city council in the summer of 1881 passed an ordinance against it. When some people voiced objection to this new ordinance, the *Daily Nugget* on August 10 carried an editorial entitled "Idiocy of Carrying Firearms":

The people who are anxious to assert their constitutional right to bear arms ought to do it openly. The revolutionary fathers, who put this into the bill of rights, did not go around with little pistols concealed in their hip pockets; they carried their rifles or muskets over their shoulders like men. If this be thought inconvenient in these undegenerate modern days, there is nothing to prevent the adoption of the old Texan plan of carrying a brace of pistols and a knife or two in the belt. Or a neat modern breech-loading carbine might be worn gracefully slung over the shoulder by an embroidered strap, thus combining the ornamental and the useful. There are numerous ways of carrying arms that are much more picturesque than the hip-pocket plan and that might not come under the ban of the Mayor, who rightly lays stress upon the word "concealed." If it is the proud right of a freeman to bear arms, why should he conceal them?

Most of the miners in Tombstone were familiar with the system of justice meted out in mining camps across the West. In these, jails were few, and so when the criminal element became too bold and the regular authorities unable to enforce security of person and property the miners would band together to reestablish justice. Their sentences to malefactors were few in number: hanging in severe cases, flogging in less severe circumstances, and banishment for minor infractions. Certainly there were elements of this frontier code in the workings of Tombstone justice in the six or seven years the town boomed. For example, a man charged with passing counterfeit money was brought before the justice of the peace in Tombstone; the evidence showed him guilty whereupon the judge "appealed to the audience, consisting mostly of hardboiled miners, to give him a severe lesson. That meant that the guilty party must leave town and keep going. So a lane was formed, and at the given word the criminal was ordered to start going. As he hurried down the lane he was 'helped along' by kicks and slaps which left him almost a wreck before he managed to disappear down the highway leading to elsewhere." John P. Gray, whose father was the justice of the peace, concluded about this case, "So far as known he never came back and passing bad money was not considered a paying business thereafter."[2]

Yet it was not characters such as this who would give Tombstone its reputation of being a town that "had a man for breakfast every morning." Rather that came from two, possibly three factions within the county. Living outside town was what became known as the "Cowboys." These principally were rustlers, along with a few genuine cattlemen who would join in a foray promising a little money. The geography and political boundaries of southeastern Arizona favored their residence, as did the paucity of law enforcement officials. Only a few miles to the south was Sonora; a few more miles to the southeast was the Mexican state of Chihuahua; and just to the east was New Mexico. Thus a criminal had four political jurisdictions, two American and two Mexican, to which he could move when pursuit came. And Mexican officials of that day, still angry at what to them had seemed American thievery of territory during the war three decades previously, were not happy to cooperate with gringo officials.

Thus at the time of the silver strike at Tombstone in 1878, there was already a considerable population of criminals—and part-time criminals—to the south and southeast of the diggings. They made their living by stealing cattle and horses in Mexico to sell in the United States to ranchers not worried by hazy titles of ownership. And lucrative contracts could be secured from the Bureau of Indian Affairs to supply beef to nearby reservations, such as San Carlos, which in 1881 alone bought 3,500,000 pounds of meat; moreover, the army bought the same commodity for the soldiers stationed in the vicinity. And horses could be sold easily to newcomers and drifters in Arizona. When Mexican officials became too efficient in pursuit of rustlers, the cowboys simply reversed the process, stealing from Americans to sell to Mexican ranchers—who similarly asked few questions about title to cattle bearing American brands. The boom at Tomstone meant only that there was a new market: supplying beef to the miners.

The number of such stealing cowboys varied with the official making the estimate. The sheriff of Cochise county gave their number at 15 to 25; the deputy United States marshal at Tucson, Joseph Evans, produced the startling estimate of 380; Acting Governor John J. Gosper probably came closest to the truth when he reported that there were about 100 cowboys and that the number rose on occasion when part-time legitimate ranchers joined in the stealing.[3] Those ranchers in the San Pedro Valley who were honest could do nothing about the situation, for a protest to law enforcement officials usually resulted in the complainer's stock being stolen—or worse. And there were more than rumors that some of the officers of the law were dishonest; for example, the *Epitaph* on December 19, 1881, commented that one horse thief had received word of his impending arrest from a deputy sheriff: "If this report is true," editorialized John Clum, "it does not speak well for Sheriff [John] Behan's judgment. . . ." The sheriff responded that it was

Newman H. Clanton, leader of the "Cowboy" faction. *Courtesy Arizona Historical Society.*

impossible to get honest ranchers to cooperate in tracking down the malefactors.

Smuggling was yet another rich source of income for the cowboys. That and the robbing of smugglers. The proximity of the Mexican border, the unsettled political condition of Mexico, and the customs duties levied both by Mexico and the United States, in combination with the geography of the San Pedro Valley, made this area a smugglers' and rustlers' paradise. Mountains to the east, mountains to the west, the Sierra Madre in Mexico, the valley a funnel leading southward, innumerable canyons where stolen herds could be held with good water and pasture, and countless trails crossing the international boundary far from the prying eyes of the few officials on either side of the line: these favored the activities of both thieves and smugglers.

Perhaps best known among the cowboy leaders was N. H. "Old Man" Clanton, who with his three sons, Joseph Isaac (Ike), Phineas, and William, had fled from Texas to California and then to Arizona. Their headquarters was a ranch house close to Lewis Springs a few miles from Charleston. Serving as a lieutenant under Old Man Clanton, and after his death as leader of the gang, was William Brocius Graham, better known as Curly Bill. Working with them was John Ringgold, called Johnny Ringo; a cousin of the infamous Younger Brothers, Ringo was a Missouri refugee by way of Texas. Near the Clanton ranch was another stronghold they often used, the ranch of Frank and Tom McLowry (also spelled McLoury). From these two ranch houses the gang could muster a score and more of followers, while a few independent organizations had smaller followings.

It was a raid on Mexican smugglers that caused the death of Old Man Clanton. In August 1881 a pack train of some fifteen Mexican smugglers, led by Miguel Garcia, was wending its way through the Peloncillo Mountains when it was attacked, reportedly by the Clantons, Curly Bill, and their gang. According to letters received by Acting Governor Gosper, three Mexicans were killed in the affair; however, the Mexican government in protesting the attack to the State Department asserted that nine Sonorans were missing. The loot consisted of coins, silver bullion, horses, cattle, and mescal to the value of approximately $4000. A few days after this raid, on the morning of August 13, Old Man Clanton and some of his men were driving cattle from New Mexico to Tombstone when they were ambushed in Guadalupe Canyon; their attackers probably were members of a unit of regular Mexican troops from the fort at Fronteras. Five of the cowboys, including Old Man Clanton, were killed in the shooting. This violence would lead to further killings on both sides of the border. Deputy United States Marshal Evans in Tucson, when sent questions from Washington about the incident, replied that the cause was 200 to 300 cowboys who lived in Mexico and that he could do nothing about it without instructions, while Governor Gosper declared that the Mexicans were as guilty of rustling and murder as were the Americans.[4]

President Chester A. Arthur took note of the troubles along the international boundary in his message to Congress on December 6, 1881, stating that these incidents of outlawry were complicating relations between the United States and Mexico. Yet, said he, the scant population of the region precluded civil authorities from raising posses for pursuit. He noted, however, that there were units of the United States Army stationed nearby, and he suggested that these troops be employed in Arizona and elsewhere as a *posse comitatus*. Yet a Democratic Congress in 1878 had passed a rider on the appropriation bill that year forbidding the use of troops in such a capacity, and the army subsequently had not been so used. Arthur in 1881 wanted such authorization, but Congress refused it. Thus the army could not legally be used to end the disturbances in southern Arizona although the President wished to do so.[5]

Meanwhile, two factions were growing in Tombstone, each claiming that the other was allied with the cowboys. These factions developed out of the contest for the office of sheriff of Cochise County, a post that was filled by the governor when the county was created in 1881. One contender for this position was John H. Behan, a former Missourian who had moved to Arizona in 1863. A

Democrat, he had served as recorder and sheriff of Yavapai County before moving to Pima County to become a deputy to Sheriff Charles Shibell. When Tombstone began to boom, Behan moved there to become a partner with John O. Dunbar in the Dexter Livery Stable and, said his enemies, a silent crony of the cowboys. Behan, by some account a "good fellow," liked to sit in a poker game with professional gamblers such as Napa Nick, and they in turn liked to have him sit in because he generally had money.

Behan's rival for the position of sheriff of Cochise County was a republican and a candidate of the "law and order" party, Wyatt Berry Stapp Earp. He and his brothers, along with a few assorted followers, constituted a curious group of would-be peace officers. Jim Earp was a saloonkeeper and professional gambler; Morgan was a gambler, gunman, and laborer; Virgil had driven a stage, ranched, prospected, and tried his hand as a peace officer; Warren was a youth barely in his twenties, but he thirsted to imitate his brothers as a gunman; and Wyatt, saloonkeeper, cardsharp, policeman, bigamist, church deacon, confidence man, and extrovert. Wyatt was the driving force behind the Earp faction, and it was he who would receive the "glory" for what followed; yet it also was he who was responsible for the failure of the Earps in Tombstone.

Wyatt Earp was born in Monmouth, Illinois, on March 19, 1848, but his father, Nicholas Porter Earp, moved to Iowa shortly thereafter, and even talked of going to California. The Civil War intervened, however, with three of his older sons, Newton, James, and Virgil, enlisting in the Union Army, Jim was wounded in 1863, permanently disabled by a bullet in his shoulder. In 1864 the family did move to San Bernardino, California. Wyatt left there in 1869 to make his way to Lamar, Missouri, where Newton lived— and to run successfully against his brother for the position of town marshal. Then on January 10, 1870, he married. His wife died a few months later and Wyatt, after quarreling with her family, drifted into Kansas. There followed a stint of buffalo hunting (in violation of Indian treaty) before he drifted through the cattle boom town of Wichita in 1874. During these years he became a cardsharp, a

Wyatt Earp. *Courtesy Arizona Historical Society.*

man with narrow face and drooping mustache who dressed in fancy white shirts. He did serve briefly as a city policeman in Wichita (from April 21, 1875, to April 19, 1876), but on April 5, 1876, he was arrested and fined for violating the peace; then two weeks later he was fired. Furthermore, a month after this incident the city commission went on record as recommending that the vagrancy laws be enforced against him and his brother Jim, who had been driving a hack in the city.

Wyatt next drifted to Dodge City where he served twice as a city policeman: from May to September 1876 and from July to November 1877. His most noteworthy exploit in July 1877 was to brawl with a dance hall girl named Frankie Bell, for which he was fined one dollar. Briefly he went to Texas but returned to Dodge City in 1878 to become an assistant marshal from May to September 1879. At one time he was a church deacon in the Union Church of Dodge City while he supplemented his income by working as a gambler.

Among the friends Earp acquired in Dodge City were such notables as William Barclay Masterson, known as "Bat." He had been a buffalo hunter—and troublemaker—before winning election as sheriff of Ford County, wherein Dodge City was located, in November 1877. And there was Luke Short, proprietor of the Long Branch Saloon whose mean temper and willingness to kill made him deadly. And there was Wyatt's best friend, Doc Holliday. Tall, slender, blond, and tubercular, John Henry Holliday was a native of Georgia and a graduate of a dentistry college. When he contracted chronic pulmonary tuberculosis, he moved to Texas in search of a cure from the dry climate, and there he had earned his living by gambling. Several arrests at Fort Griffin, Texas, led to a move to Denver, and then in 1877 he arrived in Dodge City, by then an alcoholic, with a girl in tow—Big Nosed Kate Elder, who possibly was his wife.

In 1879 Masterson failed in his bid for reelection as sheriff, and the entire Earp gang decided to move west. Going with Wyatt was young Mattie Blaylock, whom he apparently had married secretly,

Doc Holliday. *Courtesy Arizona Historical Society.*

and Doc Holliday and Big Nosed Kate. Morgan and the others were to follow, all to join Virgil and his wife Allie, who had moved to Arizona to settle near Prescott in 1876. Reunited, the Earps stopped in Tucson long enough to get Virgil a commission as a deputy United States marshal on November 27, 1879, with the duty of aiding L. F. Blackburn, who then was the deputy in Tombstone. They arrived in the town on December 1, hoping soon to make a fortune.

The first order of business was to get one of their number made a peace officer of some type. But there were only two such jobs in town, the city marshal and the deputy sheriff of Pima County, and both jobs already were held. For a time Wyatt did hold one of them, for he was appointed a deputy by Sheriff Charles Shibell. This was a lucrative position, too, for the deputy got to keep a percentage of the taxes he collected. Suddenly, however, Sheriff Shibell dismissed Wyatt and appointed John Behan the deputy, thereby starting a hatred between these two men. Wyatt thereupon went to work as a shotgun messenger for Wells, Fargo and Company, guarding strongboxes on stagecoaches—strongboxes which held other people's money.

The next several months were dull and frustrating one for the Earp gang. Virgil and the others were unable to secure work, and if it were not for their wives making money sewing they might have been forced to go to work. Then on October 27, 1880, came a break. The original town marshal, Fred White, needed help that evening when a group of the cowboys, in town drinking, began firing their pistols. White deputized Virgil Earp to help him, and the two of them managed to corner Curly Bill Brocius; in the struggle, however, Curly Bill's pistol was accidently fired, killing White. The city council on October 28 appointed Virgil to the office of city marshal; he was to serve until January, with a special election to be held on November 13 to fill the post. In that contest Virgil lost to Ben Sippy by a vote of 311 to 259; angered, Virgil resigned on November 15.

More and more of the gang were arriving, however, and some-

Virgil Earp. *Courtesy Arizona Historical Society.*

thing had to be done if they hoped to profit. In fact, all five brothers were there, along with Doc Holliday, Luke Short, and Bat Masterson. Another member of the gang was Frank Leslie, who had acquired the nickname Buckskin from his habit of habitually wearing a fringed shirt of that material and who reportedly was a crack shot. When the census of 1880 was taken, the Earp fortunes were at such low ebb that Wyatt and Virgil had listed their occupations as "farmer" and Jim had called himself a saloonkeeper. But a break came when Lou Rickabaugh, owner of the gambling concession at the Oriental Saloon, offered Wyatt a job keeping order in the establishment. Wyatt accepted, and soon Morgan Earp and Luke Short, along with Buckskin Frank Leslie, were dealing faro at the Oriental.

The next major event to occur was the regular election, held on January 4, 1881. Again Virgil was a candidate for city marshal, and again he was defeated by Ben Sippy. However, the Earp crowd could rejoice after this election, for the mayor elected that day was Republican John P. Clum; going into office with him by a landslide was a full slate of his fellow party members. And Clum was a staunch admirer of Wyatt Earp and of the Earp brothers. Clum later wrote, "The Earp brothers . . . tall, gaunt, intrepid . . . caused considerable comment when they first arrived, particularly because of Wyatt's reputation as a peace officer in Dodge City, Kansas. . . ."[6] In truth the two men, Wyatt Earp and John Clum, found looking at one another was like looking in the mirror in some respects; both were extroverts looking for the admiration of the crowd, and both were flawed in their judgment of character.

Then came the creation of Cochise County, which meant that the governor of the territory could name the first slate of county officials to serve until the next regular elections. At this time John Charles Frémont, a Republican, was the governor of Arizona. Clum and his fellow Tombstone Republicans supported Wyatt Earp for the office of county sheriff, a position Wyatt badly wanted; not only did it carry the protection of a badge for himself and his fellow gamblers, but it also meant an income of $30,000 to $40,000 in fees for collecting the county's taxes (the mining corporations and the Southern Pacific were the major taxpayers, and they paid without causing any real expenditure of time or money in securing what they owed). Wyatt Earp, with the backing of Clum and the local Republicans, had every reason to believe he would be named to the office, but Governor Frémont for some unknown reason—possibly because most of the residents of Tombstone actually were Democrats—named Democrat John Behan sheriff. Thus Earp and Behan had yet a second reason to hate one another.

Then on March 15, 1881, came an attempted robbery of the Wells, Fargo strongbox on the Kinnear stage, an event that caused great difficulty for the Earp gang. That evening the stage left Tombstone to make the run north to Benson, some twenty-five miles away, there to connect with the Southern Pacific. Reports later would state that the stage contained $80,000 in silver, a ridiculous estimate inasmuch as that much silver, according to the price then being paid, would have weighed enough to break the axle of any stagecoach of that day. Probably the amount was approximately $25,000—which was more than enough to attract the attention of many robbers.

Near Drew's Ranch, six miles north of Contention City, a deep draw crossed the road, one whose banks were so steep that the horses pulling the stage could go up the far side only at a walk. There three men burst out firing, killing driver Bud Philpot and a passenger, Peter Roerig, and shouting "Hands up!" As Philpot fell, the shotgun rider, Bob Paul, grabbed the reins and laid the whip on the horses. Paul was a veteran Wells, Fargo man who did not intend to let anyone hold him up—and he did not. The horses broke into a run up the grade, and then through a combination of good driving and good luck Paul was able to get away from the robbers. The holdup men did fire several volleys at the departing stage, but Paul reached Benson safely, his strongbox intact. Two men aboard had been killed. Later it turned out that Paul had exchanged places with driver Philpot only moments before the holdup, a trivial thing but one which saved his life; obviously that first shot, which felled Philpot, was intended for Paul.

Naturally a posse formed to track down the robbers. In this posse rode the Earps (Wyatt, Virgil, and Morgan); Marshall Williams, the Tombstone agent for Wells, Fargo and a close friend of Wyatt Earp's; and assorted other members of the Earp gang, including Bat Masterson and Frank Leslie. Also in the posse were members of the rival Behan faction, including the sheriff and his deputy William "Billy" Breakenridge.[7] At the scene of the crime they found discarded disguises, spent rifle cartridges, and tracks that led to the Redfield ranch. Len and Hank Redfield were friends of the Clantons', and it was on their place that the posse found Luther King hiding. Under questioning, King admitted holding the horses during the holdup and named Jim Crane, Harry Head, and Bill Leonard as the men who had attempted the robbery. King was returned to the Tombstone jail, but to the great embarrassment of Sheriff Behan he soon made his escape, not to be seen again.[8]

The problem for the Earps was that rumors soon spread about the town that the man who had shot Philpot was none other than Doc Holliday. The tubercular dentist had been out of town, mysteriously riding a race horse, but he claimed merely to have been engaged in a card game at Charleston. However, it was widely known that Holliday and Bill Leonard were close friends. Moreover, the rumors grew to include Wyatt Earp as planner of the robbery and Marshall Williams as the inside man who tipped off the Earp gang of the shipment. The Earps were in a frenzy to catch—some say kill—the three robbers and thereby to clear their names. Then came greater blows to the Earp hopes. Luke Short, who had shot Charles Storms in front of the Oriental Saloon on February 25, was acquitted in Tucson of the killing, but he departed the territory—as did Bat Masterson, who suddenly found himself needed in Dodge City.

Wyatt Earp thereupon approached Ike Clanton about a plan to kill the three robbers. He promised Clanton the reward money (Wells, Fargo had placed $2000 on the head of each, "Dead or Alive") if the cowboys would aid in trapping the three men. Clanton later testified that he refused, for he knew from conversations with Holliday that the dentist was the real murderer of Philpot. Gradually, however, the talk died down, even after Holliday was

Sheriff John Behan. *Courtesy Arizona Historical Society.*

fined for making threats against a man's life and then on May 30 indicted for participation in a minor shooting scrape in town. He remained free, however, if in ill humor.

Then the breaks started going the Earp way. On June 6 Ben Sippy left town, whereupon Mayor Clum and his "Law and Order" town council appointed Virgil the city marshal. On June 22 came the first of Tombstone's disastrous fires, an event that gave people something other than the stage robbery to talk about. And that same day at Eureka, New Mexico, Bill Leonard and Harry Head were killed while trying to rob the Haslett Brothers' Store, which caused Jim Crane to lead a party of cowboys to New Mexico and kill the Hasletts in return.[9] This affray left only Jim Crane to identify Holliday as the killer of Bud Philpot—with the exception of Big Nosed Kate, who knew where her husband had been that evening. And Kate was ready to talk. The *Daily Nugget*, the Democratic paper, jubilantly announced the result on July 6: "A warrant was sworn out yesterday before Judge Spicer for the arrest of Doc Holliday, a well-known character here, charging him with complicity in the murder of Bud Philpot . . . and he was arrested by Sheriff Behan. The warrant was issued upon the affidavit of Kate Elder, with whom Holliday has been living for some time past." Judge Wells Spicer, who likewise was friendly with the Earps and a member of the Republican Law and Order crowd, promptly released Holliday on bond.

The Earps retaliated by asserting that Kate was under the influence of Sheriff Behan and that she had signed the paper while drunk. At the hearing, Holliday swore he had been in Charleston playing poker and had returned to Tombstone before the time of the holdup. Wyatt Earp testified that he had seen the dentist in town at the time and that at ten that evening he had told Holliday of the attempted robbery, whereupon Holliday had ridden out to help. Thus he was seen by reliable witnesses riding in the area. The case was dismissed. On July 9, Virgil Earp arrested Kate for drunken and disorderly conduct, and she was fined $12.50. Kate thus realized that Tombstone was no longer safe for her, and she departed immediately, moving to Globe, Arizona, where she opened a boarding house.[10]

Several other events were transpiring that summer which were to have a bearing on subsequent events. One was the rivalry between Wyatt Earp and Sheriff Behan for the affections of an "actress" called Sadie. She had met Behan in Prescott and had followed him to Tombstone, hoping he would divorce his wife and marry her. In Tombstone she met Wyatt, who likewise fell in love and began courting her, notwithstanding his marriage to Mattie Blaylock. Wyatt began polishing his boots and wearing his fanciest white shirts, openly taking Sadie to Tombstone's best restaurants—to the chagrin of Sheriff Behan.[11] The same summer the Clantons were ambushed by Mexicans and the patriarch of the clan was killed. Moreover, there were several additional stage robberies, all of which occurred when a heavy shipment of silver was leaving town. And the Earp brothers one by one found it necessary to leave town with heavy suitcases to visit their parents in Colton, California.

On September 8, 1881, there was yet another stage robbery, this one out of the ordinary. It was the Bisbee stage, and it had $2500 aboard in the Wells, Fargo strongbox. At 11 p.m. two masked bandits halted it, taking the Wells, Fargo money and $750 in cash and jewelry from the passengers. But the driver overheard one of the bandits ask the other if they had taken all the "sugar," meaning loot. When this story was repeated in town, several people recognized this as a favorite word of T. C. "Frank" Stilwell, formerly a deputy of Sheriff Behan's. Two posses rode out to track down the robbers, one led by Behan and his deputies, Breakenridge and Dave Neagle, the other consisting of Wyatt and Morgan Earp along with Marshall Williams and Fred Dodge (both Wells, Fargo employees). Behan and his group arrested Stilwell and Pete Spence, who owned the Bisbee Livery Stable with Stilwell and who was a known friend of Wyatt and Virgil Earp's. The Earps then arrived, and after Marshall Williams swore out a warrant against the men for robbing the mails, Deputy United States Marshal Virgil Earp arrested them on that charge. Thus both posses brought in the prisoners, only to have them released on bond.

Wyatt Earp began spreading the rumor around town that the Clanton gang was angry at having two of its members arrested and that the other cowboys were making threats on his and his brothers' lives. According to one version of the events that followed, the Earps were still smarting over the accusation that they were the instigators of the stage robbery and killing in March and had decided to arrange another where they could be heroes. Reportedly they went to Ike Clanton and asked him to get some of his men and stage a holdup whereat the Earps and Doc Holliday would save the day—with no one getting hurt or arrested. But Ike feared that he and his men would be shot in the fake holdup and began telling everyone in town of the Earps' suggestion. In truth, the Clantons knew who was behind many of the robberies, which had caused Wyatt to decide they had to be eliminated. Later, reliable witnesses would tell widely divergent stories as to the origins of the feud, both as to its causes, who were the villains, and who the instigators.

The fight occurred on October 26. On the twenty-fifth Ike Clanton and Tom McLowry went into town for supplies. Holliday met Ike in a restaurant and tried to provoke a fight, but Ike was not armed. That evening in a poker game that included Sheriff Behan, Ike and Virgil exchanged hot words. The next morning Virgil and Morgan, whom Marshal Virgil had deputized, found Ike Clanton armed; after Virgil disarmed Clanton, he hit him over the head with the barrel of his gun and dragged him into court where Clanton was fined twenty-five dollars for violating the town ordinance against carrying weapons. That same morning Wyatt met the unarmed Tom McLowry and hit him in the face, leaving him in the gutter bleeding.

Meanwhile Billy Clanton and Frank McLowry had gone to town. Frank emerged from a store to find Wyatt, also deputized by his brother, jerking the McLowry horse around by the bit. When Frank complained, Wyatt told him to keep the animal in the road and off the sidewalk. Frank took his horse down to the OK Corral, and he and his friends continued to go about town doing errands and making purchases. Wyatt, Morgan, and Virgil, together with Doc

SAFFORD STREET

FREMONT STREET

ALLEN STREET

TOUGH-NUT STREET

MOUNTAIN MAID MINE

FIRE RUINS

RUINS

COMBINATION MINE

MINERS CABINS

2ND STREET
3RD STREET
4TH STREET
5TH STREET
6TH STREET

1 Cochise County Courthouse
2 Tombstone City Hall
3 Episcopal Church
4 Tombstone Epitaph Office
5 Crystal Palace Saloon
6 Oriental Saloon
7 Bird Cage Theatre
8 Fire House
9 Schieffelin Hall
10 OK Corral

A Curly Bill shot
Marshal Fred White 1881

B OK Corral Fight—
Billy Clanton,
Frank & Tom McLowery
shot by the Earps 1881

C Virgil Earp ambushed
and wounded 1881

D Morgan Earp assassinated 1882

MAP 3 Street Map of Tombstone

Holliday, were standing in front of Hafford's Saloon watching. By this time it was one-thirty in the afternoon, and word was spreading around town that the Earps and the cowboys were going to settle their feud.

According to a pro-Earp version of what followed, Sheriff Behan went up to the brothers and Holliday and said, "It's all right boys. I've disarmed them."

"Did you arrest them?" Virgil wanted to know.

Told no, the Earps started toward the corral, whereupon the sheriff retreated into photographer C. S. Fly's studio to hide. When the two groups came together in the street in front of the corral, Virgil reportedly stated, "You men are under arrest. Throw up your hands." But the cowboys went for their guns, and shots were fired. Behan, according to this account, had lied about disarming the cowboys. Virgil was wounded, but raised his cane as if to say, "We didn't want that."[12]

Several far more reliable witnesses tell a vastly different story, however. Sheriff Behan later testified that he tried to disarm the McLowrys, Ike and Billy Clanton, and young Billy Claibourne. According to the sheriff, Ike Clanton and Tom McLowry were unarmed, and Billy Claibourne said he was merely trying to get the cowboys out of town. Another witness was John P. Gray, who stated, "I saw the battle." His account was:

The three Earps—Wyatt, Virgil and Morgan—and Doc Holliday had stepped suddenly out on to Fremont Street from the rear entrance of the OK stable lot and immediately commenced firing on the . . . cowboys who were preparing to leave town; in fact Frank McLowery was sitting on his horse and at first fire fell mortally wounded, but game to the last he returned the fire wounding Virgil Earp in the arm, leaving that member useless for any further gunplays in the life of Virgil Earp. The other two cowboys lay dead in the street. Tom McLowery had his hands up when a load of buckshot cut him down. It was all over almost as soon as begun. A play enacted by the Earps to wipe out those cowboys under the pretense of enforcing the law—and carried out under the manner of shooting first and reading the warrant to the dead men afterward. But in this case I doubt if there was ever a warrant issued. The Earps called out, "Hands up" and began firing almost simultaneously.[13]

All witnesses agree that the battle was short. In 1931 John Clum recalled, "I had just gone to my room to change my clothing, when crack-crack-crack, the guns let loose down at the corral. Before I could turn the corner it was all over. The dead and the wounded were carried away by friends."[14] Some said the shooting lasted only fifteen seconds; others claimed thirty. However long the duration, the cowboys definitely came out second best in the affair: Tom and Frank McLowry were dead, along with Billy Clanton. Virgil and Morgan Earp were seriously wounded, while Doc Holliday was grazed by a bullet.

Sheriff Behan moved immediately to arrest his opponents, the Earp faction. Virgil and Morgan were so incapacitated that there was no thought of arresting them, but they were so fearful of some sort of reprisal that they forted up in Virgil's house; they locked the doors, put matresses in front of the windows, and sat heavily armed all evening. The next day warrants were obtained for the arrests of Wyatt, Virgil, and Morgan Earp and Doc Holliday. Brought before Judge Wells Spicer, they had a full hearing that lasted through November. The decision, handed down December 1, was long— and partisan; he found the evidence insufficient to warrant holding the defendants for trial, and they were released. Because the testimony presented during the trial had strongly shown the murderous intent of the Earps and had indicated that most of the cowboys were unarmed except for saddle guns—all of which had been fully presented in the columns of the *Nugget*—that newspaper editorialized on December 1 that ". . . In the eyes of many the Justice [Wells Spicer] does not stand like Caesar's wife, 'Not only virtuous but above suspicion.' "

The coroner's report of his investigation of the bodies stated, "From the body of Thos McLowry, I recovered in certificates of

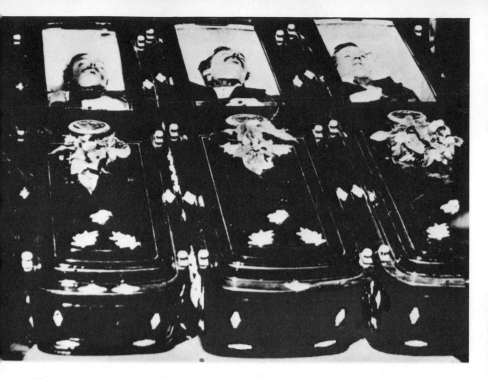

The aftermath of the Gunfight at the OK Corral. As these bodies were taken to the cemetery, local residents draped a banner over the caskets proclaiming, "Murdered in the Streets of Tombstone." *Courtesy Arizona Historical Society.*

deposit in the Pima County Bank, checks and cash in all the sum of $2943.45—From the body of Frank McLowry one Colts six shooting pistol, with belt and cartridges.—From the body of William Clanton, one Colts six shooter, with belt and cartridges and one nickel watch and chain."[15] Some questioned where these pistols had come from inasmuch as witnesses testified that the two men had not been armed.

The result of this shooting was immediate. Virgil Earp was suspended from his office as city marshal. And the miners of the town turned viciously on the Earps to support the cowboys and Sheriff Behan. When the three dead men were buried in one of the best-attended funerals in the history of Tombstone, a banner was draped on the caskets proclaiming, "Murdered in the Streets of Tombstone." And a "Citizens' Safety Committee," originally organized by the Law and Order faction of Republicans, likewise turned against the violent Earps, telling them that in the future such shootings would result in hangings without benefit of Judge Wells Spicer and his court. George Parsons returned to town the following day, and he noted in his diary:

> Much excitement in town and people apprehensive and scary. A bad time yesterday when Wyatt, Virgil, and Morgan Earp with Doc Holiday [sic] had a street fight with the two McLowerys and Bill Clanton and Ike, all but the latter being killed and V and M Earp wounded. Desperate men and a desperate encounter. Bad blood had been brewing some time and I was not surprised at the outbreak. It is only a wonder it has not happened before. . . . The "Stranglers" [vigilantes] were out in force and showed sand. . . . Loud talking or talking in groups was tho't out of place. Had to laugh at some of the nervousness. It has been a bad scare and the worst is not yet over some think.[16]

Indeed the worst was not over, although Morgan and Virgil Earp did recover from their wounds. Yet they stood in extreme danger of receiving more wounds, possibly fatal ones, for rumors of a death list began circulating about Tombstone after December 1 and the decision to release the Earp faction. The *Epitaph* published one written to Wells Spicer; indeed the *Epitaph* might publish it, for editor John Clum's name likewise was on it:

> To Wells Spicer:—Sir, if you take my advice you will take your Departure for a more genial Clime, as I don't think this is Healthy for you any longer. If Sons of Bitches as you Are allowed to dispense Justice in this Territory, the sooner you Depart from us the better for yourself And the community at large you may make light of this But it is only a matter of time you get it sooner or later So with those few gentle hints I will conclude for the first and Last time.
>
> A Miner[17]

This threat was not idle, for on December 14, 1881, Clum was fired upon three miles out of town, as he was leaving town by stagecoach for the East.[18] Exactly two weeks later Virgil Earp was shot from ambush and received a crippling wound from which he would never fully recover. Other disasters hit the Earps, one of which was Wyatt being forced to give up his interest in the Oriental Saloon's gambling concession. Gradually the gang began to divest itself of its mining properties and its town lots (no one knew how they had been acquired).

Then on March 18, 1882, Morgan was fatally shot from ambush as he was playing pool at Campbell and Hatch's Saloon. Wyatt was an eye-witness to the assassination.[19] Questioning revealed that it was probably Frank Stilwell, aided by Indian Charlie, who had done it. The coroner's verdict also named Pete Spence and a man named Freis as being party to the murder. Indian Charlie was captured on the day of the inquest. Two days after the murder the injured Virgil and his wife left Tombstone, taking Morgan's body to be buried at the home of their parents at Colton, California.

Accompanying them as far as Tucson was Wyatt and Warren Earp, along with Doc Holliday, Sherman McMasters, and Turkey Creek Jack Johnson. Just as the train bearing Morgan's body departed, guns roared in the railroad yards. Wyatt had found Frank Stilwell, and by self-admission he shot Stilwell—who had not drawn his gun. He claimed that Stilwell grabbed his pistol and that it went off; however, the newspaper the following morning stated that Stilwell's body had six shots in it, "four rifle balls and two loads of buckshot." Stilwell reportedly had gone to the trail depot to meet a witness who was to testify for him in the case against him of robbing the Bisbee stage in 1881. After this shooting, the Earp gang returned to Tombstone and lodged at the Cosmopolitan Hotel. Sheriff Behan decided to arrest them, believing that a warrant would come shortly from Tucson; in this attempt he enlisted the aid of his former deputy, Dave Neagle, who had been elected town marshal in the election of January 3, 1882. But Neagle wanted no part of Behan's plot; instead he went to the Earps and reportedly told them, "This is none of my affair, Wyatt, but the sheriff is going to arrest you and he thought maybe if I talked to you, you could save some trouble."[20]

Actually the Earps had not been in Tombstone long. They returned only to pack, get their horses, and ride out of town. Charged with murder, a warrant out for their arrest, Wyatt and Warren departed Arizona. In the process Wyatt abandoned his second wife Mattie Blaylock to whatever fate might have in store for her. Sheriff Behan followed them at a discreet distance, while Town Marshal Neagle joined Dr. Goodfellow in his ambulance to go to Chandler's Ranch. Yet another gun battle had occurred there. Some of the deputies had encountered a few of the cowboys, and shooting had resulted. Neagle arrived to discover Deputy John C. Gillespie dead, Zweig Hunt shot in the chest, Billy Grounds shot in the face, and two other men wounded. Only Deputy Breakenridge was unhurt.[21]

This violence between the Earps and the cowboys, along with the international difficulties caused by the wars between Mexican smugglers and the cowboys, caught national headlines. Tombstone certainly was gaining a reputation as a tough town—and there seemed to be no one to clean it up. Sheriff Behan was incapable, nor could the army be used. And the United States marshal for Arizona Territory, Crawley P. Dake, was incompetent. He resided in Prescott, the territorial capital, which was 250 miles from the scene of difficulty. In Prescott, Dake was managing to acquire an estate of some $22,000 during his four-year tenure of office, part of which came by dishonest means. And when anyone in the territory asked for help, Dake's response was to request money and instructions from Washington. By August 1881 his bond had been revoked because he had spent more than the amount of his bond. Nor was his deputy in Tucson, J. W. Evans, any better.[22] No aid could be expected from that quarter.

President Chester A. Arthur finally took the only step open to him. He issued a presidential proclamation on May 3, 1882, stating:

Whereas it has been made to appear . . . to me . . . [that] it
has become impracticable to enforce by the ordinary course of
judicial proceedings the laws of the United States within that
Territory [of Arizona] . . . the laws of the United States require
that whenever it may be necessary, in the judgment of the President, to use the military forces for the purpose of enforcing . . .
the laws . . . he shall forthwith, by proclamation, command
such insurgents to disperse and retire peaceably to their respective
abodes within a limited time. . . .

He ordered Arizonans to cease "aiding, countenancing, abetting or
taking part in . . . unlawful proceedings" by noon, May 15, 1882.[23]
Clearly he was threatening the use of martial law should disturbances continue to disrupt the peace.

In Cochise County the citizens reacted to the President's threat
with indignation, holding meetings in which they charged Arthur
with slandering their home. The *Epitaph*, which Clum had sold
to Democrat Sam Purdy in April that year, editorialized against
newspapers which had sensationalized Arizona; he concluded that
"there is not a State or Territory in the Union more peaceable than
Arizona, nor one in which the law is more promptly obeyed or
thoroughly respected."[24]

Public opinion had turned against the outlaws of whatever stripe.
Tombstone's residents no longer would condone outlawry—and
that, not a presidential proclamation or the departure of the Earps,
was what would bring a return to legal stability. And they were
impatient with what to them seemed the trickery of the courts, the
conniving ways of lawyers, and the reversal of justice by courts of
appeal. Thus when there seemed a possibility that true justice
might be thwarted, they were more than ready to intercede. One
of the best instances of this in Tombstone grew out of a robbery in
December 1883 in Bisbee; there a gang of amateurish thugs robbed
a store filled with Christmas shoppers and fired indiscriminately
into the crowd, killing three men and a woman. A posse quickly
formed to track down the criminals.

EXECUTION OF

DANIEL KELLY, OMER W. SAMPLE, JAS. HOWARD, DANIEL DOWD and WILLIAM DELANEY,

AT THE COURT HOUSE, TOMBSTONE, ARIZONA,

March 28, 1884, at ..*1*.... O'clock p. m.

Admit Mr. *H J Fisher*

J L Ward

NOT TRANSFERABLE.   SHERIFF.

Invitation to the hanging of the men responsible for the Bisbee Massacre. These were given by the sheriff and were highly prized, for there always were more men wanting to see executions than there was space. *Courtesy Arizona Historical Society.*

One member of that posse, a saloonkeeper named John Heath, so often tried to lead the trackers on the wrong trail that the other members grew suspicious. Under "questioning" Heath admitted that he had planned the robbery and named the perpetrators. The five actual robbers were arrested, brought to trial, and sentenced to be hanged on March 28, 1884, Red Sample, Dan Dowd, Tex Howard, Dan Kelley, and William Delaney were executed in the courtyard of the county courthouse at Tombstone. But Heath, who had not participated in the actual robbery, was sentenced only to twenty years in prison. To the residents of Bisbee this seemed a miscarriage of justice, and a vigilance committee came to Tombstone, took Heath out of jail, and hanged him to a telegraph pole on February 22, 1884. Tombstone residents approved the action—but they had a corpse unaccounted for on their hands. A coroner's jury solemnly convened and, despite a photograph showing the dead man and the crowd around him, accepted the verdict recommended by the coroner, Dr. George E. Goodfellow: "We the undersigned find that J. Heath came to his death from emphysema of the lungs—a disease common to high altitudes—which might have been caused by strangulation, self-inflicted or otherwise."[25]

By 1883, however, the day of the outlaw was passing in southern Arizona. In fact, the miners in Tombstone did not yet know it, but their town itself was on the decline. The shafts below ground were beginning to flood, the price of silver was declining, and the cattlemen in the area were organizing to drive out the rustlers. The days of unrestrained outlawry, along with the days of glory, were ending. Tombstone was on the decline.

The Decline of Tombstone

Tombstone in 1883 appeared prosperous. Few indeed were discerning enough to see the pallor of death that was descending on the city; rather most mistook the growing signs to be merely the approach of maturity. More than a thousand claims had been located and recorded, while the richness and extensiveness of the ore had caused widespread attention. Investments had poured in to such an extent that Tombstone had become one of the most important mining districts in the United States. Elaborate corporate structures had been organized, the promoters developing the unique practice of selling shares in their mines on a million-share basis rather than on the traditional foot basis. Mines had been opened in all directions until the hills were covered with hoisting works; in fact, the stranger might be led to believe that a head frame was merely some strange, local form of vegetation. Mills had been erected on the San Pedro River and even in the shadow of the town itself, bringing with them several satellite villages. And in town white-coated bartenders knew all the latest cocktails, while chefs imported from Paris prepared gourmet food. Water had been piped from the distant Huachuca Mountains, and touring theatrical troups brought the latest bits of culture from distant New York.

But something had gone out of the town, that indefinable something that gave it a unique flavor. The growth that was a symbol of progress was also a sign of the death of the spontaneous, ebullient, prankish, bubbling spirit that Tombstone had possessed back in 1879 and 1880. True, the city in 1883 had a population somewhere between 7000 and 12,000 people (depending on which estimate was accepted); trade was flourishing, both internally and with Mexico; the mines would produce approximately $2,600,000 in silver and gold that year; evidences of stability could be seen in the weekly and monthly payrolls being met, the number of men present at union meetings, the growth of church membership, the erection of more permanent schools, and the arrival of more and yet more women in the city. True, the adventurous young man could still join "The Tombstone Toughs" to fight the Apaches skulking in the hills.[1] True there were still a few exciting discoveries of silver being made. But the talk was of new mining camps in Colorado and Montana, not of local events. The miners discussed wages in the rival copper industry, no longer saving to head out on a prospect. Even the arrival of more women only heralded the loss of that adolescent male attitude which had been the hallmark of the town in its wild period.

Yes, Tombstone was a phenomenon, a seven-day wonder, its glory brief, its time in the sun only a fleeting moment to hills that had witnessed the passage of ages. No one in March 1880 realized how brief the city's garland of fame would be when Ed and Al Schieffelin decided to sell their interest in the Tombstone Mining and Milling Company. The comments for the most part were that the brothers were extremely foolish. But Ed Schieffelin was a born prospector, a restless man who could not stay in one place long even after he was rich. Late in 1879, after making arrangements for a stage company to haul the bullion to Tucson, he had been overpowered by wanderlust. ". . . I was a little disatisfied with the results of our labor," he recalled later, "and did not think we had accomplished much." Thus he wandered off in search of some new discovery, leaving his brother and Dick Gird to manage the mining operation.

Ed returned to Tombstone in February 1880 after a three-month prospect to discover that he was a much-sought man. In fact, letters and telegrams had been sent to all parts of the country seeking him. The eastern financiers wanted to purchase his and his brother's share of the company. They were so anxious that, without waiting for him to be found, they had started their journey to Tombstone. The party consisted of "Messrs. Disston, Corbin, Asbury, Hart and Sheriff Wright. . . ." They had chartered a special train car to reach the vicinity, and thus Schieffelin went to meet them in March 1880. Disston became their spokesman, and to Ed Schieffelin he put their question: what would he and his brother take for their interest in the Tough Nut Mill and Mining Company and the Corbin Mill and Mining Company?

Ed and Al discussed this proposition and finally decided they would sell their joint interest for $600,000. The financiers accepted their demands, but not for cash. The final arrangement was that the two Schieffelins would be paid $50,000 on April 1 and the remainder in monthly installments. The Tucson *Arizona Weekly Star* reported this sale was dated March 17 with the comment that the purchasers were "the Corbin brothers, the Disston party of Philadelphia, the Hulings Bros. of Oil City, Pa.; and Messrs. Simmons and Squires of Boston." Ed later recalled, "My brother went East, and held the stock in his possession until the money was paid. That closed down my own and my brother's connection with Tombstone, excepting one or two small prospects which we sold afterwards. The Graveyard we did some work on, but it did not amount to much. The Tombstone claim we sold for a few hundred dollars, and it has never turned out of much importance. Another mine close to it, called the Ground Hog, and another, the Contact, we sold, one for $6,000 and the other for $15,000 I think."[2] Thus ended the brothers' investment in Tombstone, an investment which they had procured with their sweat and at the risk of their lives.

Dick Gird did not sell his part of the companies in March 1880, however. Neither did gun dealer John Vosburg and Ex-Governor A. P. K. Safford. At least, they did not sell at that time. Safford used his profits from this and other ventures to join a syndicate of Eastern capitalists; it purchased a 4,000,000-acre tract of land in Florida on which it would found the city of Tarpon Springs. Late in 1881 Safford did return to Arizona—to marry a third time; he chose as his bride Miss Soledad Bonillas. And he apparently dis- posed of his holdings about this time, for the Tombstone *Epitaph* stated on January 12, 1882, that the ex-governor was in town, hav- ing arrived by stage from Bisbee the day before. "It is reported," said the *Epitaph* story, "that Gov. Safford has closed out all his Arizona interests, and will hereafter devote himself exclusively to the development of the gigantic reclamation and colonization schemes that he is interested in in Florida."[3] Vosburg, however, would hold onto his part of the venture until much later, taking from it sufficient money to live out his life in comfort.[4]

And Dick Gird retained his interest in the venture in Tombstone, even building an additional mill as required. The *Arizona Weekly Star* of Tucson reported on April 29, 1880, that Gird was in Tucson and that he intended to put five more stamps in the Tombstone mill, bringing the company's total to thirty stamps. The twenty-five already in operation were crushing forty-five tons of ore daily. At Millville, Gird had designed a comfortable life for himself. His office in the Tombstone Mill and Mining Company building was described by the Tucson *Arizona Citizen* on September 19, 1879, as "a model of architecture . . . [and] without question the finest building . . . in southern Arizona." Gird furnished the building in black walnut, had carpeting in his sleeping quarters, and in- stalled a fireplace to give warmth on cold nights. His youngest sister, Emily, was mistress of the household until Gird married and brought his bride there in January 1880. John Vosburg later remem- bered that Gird's wife had moved to California at age sixteen with her parents—so poor that they had to wrap their feet in rags for four weeks until they earned sufficient money to buy shoes. A de- vout Catholic, Mrs. Gird installed a shrine in the offices of the mining company.[5]

Apparently the Gird home became the social center of Millville-

Charleston, with marriages and parties taking place there. On January 8, 1881, the *Epitaph* reported "a joyous event of a social nature" occurring the previous Monday night "at the elegant Millville Villa of Mr. and Mrs. Richard Gird, the occasion being the first anniversary of their wedding." It started at eight o'clock. The guests spent an hour in "congratulations and social conversation," then adjourned to the saloon hall "and to excellent orchestra music, joined in the merry dance until the stroke of midnight, when the supper march announced the banqueting hours." A "sumptuous spread" was accompanied by toasts "in brimming goblets of choisest vintage" to the "health and long life of the fortunate couple."

Gird's salary and his dividends were mounting with sufficient rapidity that by the summer of 1880 he was looking for a major investment. This he made in September 1880: he purchased the Chino Ranch at the edge of Los Angeles County, California, for $80,000, and there he began an extensive amount of renovation. The *Phoenix Herald* on May 27, 1881, quoted from the Los Angeles *Herald* to the effect that Gird was erecting a five-wire fence around the Chino Ranch, which totaled 38,000 acress. That meant a 30-mile fence, or 150 miles of barbed wire.[6]

After the Schieffelins sold their interest in the company, Gird remained with it for another year before selling out. And when he did finally sell, he received more for his single quarter of the business than had the two Schieffelins for their combined half of it (although some reports state that he received only $600,000—or exactly the same as Ed and Al together had received). Then, with no legal or even moral obligation to do so, inasmuch as he had counseled the brothers not to sell when they did, he hunted them up and gave each sufficient money so that all three ended up with exactly the same amount. Thus the original agreement, never committed to writing, to the effect that the three would share equally in whatever was found was honored as the three men disappeared from the stage of Tombstone's history.[7] And the three parted with respect and friendship. Gird said of Al, "A better, more honest, truthful, and naturally good man it would be hard to find than was Al Schieffelin." He felt that Ed was "self-conscious, given to personal display, even worrying what others might be thinking of his comings and goings; but, at bottom, Ed in all affairs of life was honorable and true." Vosburg likewise remembered the three with fondness; at age eighty-six he stated, "All my direct associates have passed on, but a tender memory of them will always abide by and comfort me. First, the Little Governor—because I knew him the longest and best. Then, Ed, and Al, and Dick Gird, all exceptionally good men and true."[8]

Even in 1881, when Gird parted company with the firm, it seemed foolish to sell. The silver ore, also rich in gold, was holding steady the deeper the shafts went. Yet it is possible that Gird sold because he foresaw the future of the district in an event of the third week of March 1881—an event that others greeted with enthusiasm. Water was found at approximately the 500-foot level in the Sulphuret Mine. In a story headlined "Here's Richness," the *Epitaph* on March 25 stated, "This past week has been a most important one in the history of Tombstone. Water has been struck in one of the leading mines of the district, of a character to leave little doubt as to the permanency of the flow." Most experts in the area had predicted water eventually would be reached, but not until the shafts were down about 1000 feet. Thus no hoisting works had been constructed with a view to removing water from the shafts and cross-cuts.

The reason the discovery of water was considered beneficial to Tombstone was cited in the *Epitaph* story of March 25: "One well informed and very conservative mining man yesterday remarked to the *Epitaph* reporter that in his opinion the camp had been benefited 100 percent by the encountering of water in the Sulphuret. It would inspire renewed confidence in the permanency of the veins, it would relieve the mines of the expense of hauling ore so many miles to the river; it would tend to bring more capital to Tombstone district than would a dozen 'big Strikes' in the upper levels of the mines themselves." As a result of the discovery, some of the

The Girard Mill, built in Tombstone. *Courtesy Arizona Historical Society.*

companies did erect mills within sight of Tombstone, especially after the permanency of the water at the 500-foot level was proved by its discovery at a similar depth in the Contention, Grand Central, West Side, Head Center, and Empire mines. Eventually the engineers would determine that Tombstone was on a mesa nearly 4500 feet above sea level, but its water table was excessively high; only a few miles away and a few hundred feet lower, the water almost erupted from the ground in natural springs at the little Mormon settlement of St. David.

The erection of a twenty-stamp mill in Tombstone to use the water pumped from below ground meant a saving of the $3.50 a ton it was costing to freight the ore nine miles to the San Pedro River. This mill was the Girard, which used Cornish pumps to lift water from the Grand Central and Contention mines. Other pumps were installed, forcing a partial suspension of work in those two mines in 1883, but by 1884 when the new pumps began their work the water level was lowered. In the emptied shafts, stopes, and drifts, the miners again were mucking out rich ore. The success of the pumps renewed confidence in Tombstone mining, for they seemed to prove that the water could be controlled—and used to advantage.

But the times were changing at the national level. Monetary policies of the United States government, over which the mine owners and workers had no control, gradually would begin to hurt the town of Tombstone. Silver's history as a part of the monetary system of the United States had been checkered, but in 1834 had been set by Congress at a ratio of sixteen to one with gold. However, during the Civil War, the government was forced to issue paper money; after the conflict the paper money gradually was retired from circulation. And in 1873 Congress had dropped the silver dollar (except for a trade silver dollar to be used for export purposes); this dropping of silver from the monetary system was called the "Crime of '73" by Western mining interests, which brought sufficient political pressure to bear to secure passage of the Bland-Allison Act in 1878. The Bland-Allison Act, passed on February 28 (just as the boys were on the road to Tombstone), had provided for the purchase monthly of $2,000,000 to $4,000,000 in silver bullion to be coined into dollars at a ratio of sixteen to one with gold. This artificially pegged the price of silver at approximately $1.29 per ounce—until huge new discoveries of the metal were made in the West. Then the price began to decline steadily, dipping below one dollar per ounce by the mid-1880s. Gradually the marginal mines of Tombstone would succumb to the falling price of silver, and the large ones would have to fight to find ways of cutting costs.

Because of the ascendancy of the "Hard Money" crowd in Washington, the mine owners of Tombstone in 1884 cut wages from four dollars to three dollars a day. This cut had taken place at other points in the territory, especially in the copper towns, but the union in Tombstone refused to accept the reduction. On May 1 a strike resulted, during which public opinion gradually turned against the union. There even was talk that the union leaders were enriching themselves through graft; true or not, the leaders were stubborn and held out for the four-dollar-a-day wage. The companies offered a compromise at $3.50 per day; the president of the miners' union replied that he wanted a peaceful settlement, but said he feared violence if the four-dollar wage was not paid. There would be no compromise.[9]

Then on May 10 the Safford Hudson Bank of Tucson failed, and with it went its branch in Tombstone. Officials of the main branch in Tucson blamed their failure on the mining companies of Tombstone, while the officers of the branch in the mining town declared the reason for failure to be the speculations of the Tucson crowd. Whatever the reason, the failure hit Tombstone's striking miners hard. Some of them lost all their savings, and indignation was approaching the point of a full-scale riot. A federal judge and several influential citizens promised an investigation, and this—backed by a company of soldiers from Fort Huachuca and a hundred deputies sworn by the sheriff—mollified the miners sufficiently to avoid the destruction of property in Tombstone.[10]

Then rumors began to spread that the miners planned to destroy the hoisting works and other mining property at the various shafts. And the miners did seem confident of victory, for they had assurances of support from fellow unionists in Bodie, California, and Virginia City, Nevada; some outside funds did come to the union in Tombstone to help maintain the strike. Guards were maintained at all the company mines on a twenty-four-hour-a-day basis, but with the arrival of the soldiers from Fort Huachuca tempers gradually began to cool. Some of the strikers ran out of money and drifted northward to the Globe-Miami district in Arizona where copper was being mined—at three dollars a day—and some went south to Bisbee, also into the copper mines. After four months the strike ended, but its effect on Tombstone was permanent. Some of the mines never reopened; consequently still more people left town, causing a few more merchants to close their establishments.[11]

There still was rich ore below ground once the miners went back to work. The water problem was being handled by the pumps installed the year before by the Grand Central Company and the Contention Company. The Grand Central had brought a line of direct-acting steam pumps capable of raising 500,000 gallons during each twenty-four-hour period, while the Contention had put in a plant of twelve-inch Cornish pumps at a cost of $150,000 with double the capacity of the Grand Central's pumps. Then, when the shafts pushed lower and lower and the water was not receding rapidly enough, the Grand Central owners installed Cornish pumps capable of emptying 1,500,000 gallons every twenty-four hours; the cost was $200,000 for the new machinery, but it seemed a wise investment when the water again receded at a satisfactory rate and mining could continue. Even while the mines were shut down for the installation of this machinery, however, the two companies had continued to pay dividends to their stockholders out of their cash reserves. No company official sufficiently understood the seriousness of the problem facing them.[12]

Even after the strike had been settled and the water was receding, there was a gradual diminution of the mining activity in the district. The declining price of silver was forcing one operation after another to suspend its work. Thus there was a corresponding loss of employment at the reduction works at Charleston, for what ore was being brought out was being crushed at the Tombstone mills to save the cost of transportation. The gradual strangulation of Charleston was reflected in the number of registered voters, which declined from a high of 173 in 1882 to 118 in 1884 to 60 in 1886.[13] Then in May 1886 the two concentrating works at Charleston were dismantled to be moved elsewhere, and the town was doomed. Then came an earthquake on May 3, 1887, which cracked the walls of many of the buildings, most of which were already deserted. And the post office was moved to Fairbank, six miles down the San Pedro, on October 24, 1888. That signaled the end. A reporter for the Tombstone *Prospector* reported on June 14, 1889, that the former city "has been given over to the Mexican population, who live in tents and houses claimed by no one." He said that doors and roofs, even room partitions, had been ripped out of many of the houses to be burned as firewood by drifting cowboys and the few residents, and concluded by stating, "The only news that comes from that direction now is brought by some

Charleston as a ghost town. *Courtesy Arizona Historical Society.*

passerby on his way from some of the ranches in the Huachuca Mountains."[14]

The pumping continued in Tombstone as men fought valiantly to reach the rich ore still being mined below the natural water level. Downward, slowly downward the water receded, reluctant to reveal the treasure it had inundated for so many centuries; still it flowed although enough seemingly was pumped up to satisfy a Noah. By the time the water had receded to the 600-foot level— that was early in 1886—the mining engineers were convinced that they were tapping a basin which, when drained, could be held at the same level indefinitely with only moderate additional pumping needed. At both the Contention and the Grand Central, vertical shafts had been pushed down to the water level; and from these vertical shafts, cross-cuts reached out to the ore bodies. At the Contention, for example, the ore coming up from that level was assaying at $100 to the ton in gold alone.

Then on May 12, 1886, came yet another blow. Mrs. J. H. Macia later would recall the day: "We heard the fire whistles early one morning and hurried out of the house." She saw people screaming and pointing toward the Grand Central; others merely were standing in the dusty street looking—and some were crying. A glance up the hill told Mrs. Macia the cause of the uproar, "I remember how the draft from the shaft blew a column of flame and smoke high in the air. You could hear it roar."[15] That fire destroyed both the hoisting works and the water pumps, the latter alone valued at $350,000. The pumps still working at the Contention could have held the water in check until new pumps could have been erected at the Grand Central, but the two companies began to argue with each other about the costs involved, costs which other mine owners in the vicinity refused to help shoulder although all obviously would benefit from the removal of the water.

The arguing continued, but the pumps did not. The owners of the Contention simply shut down their pumps to prevent the miners in the Grand Central from bringing up ore. Obviously the officials of the Contention did not intend to shoulder the entire cost of draining the Tombstone district. And the result was a gradual climb of the water level—which became permanent when yet another fire occurred. The *Epitaph* graphically recorded the scene at the Contention:

At about 1 o'clock Sunday morning a small blaze was seen by a few persons in town whose attention was drawn toward Contention Hill. At first it was thought that a small cabin was on fire and it was not known to be in the magnificent hoisting works of the Contention mine. The alarm was sounded at the three houses of the fire department in the city, but no assistance could be given by dragging the hose carts up there, a mile distant. . . . It was 45 minutes before the immense structure was enveloped in flame from ground to apex of the main building. The picture was sublime as well as awful to contemplate. Nothing could be done to stop the progress of the flames.

Sparks from the fire dropped into the shaft and ignited the timbers underground, sending up "flame a hundred feet in the air, resembling the burning of gas over a natural gas well."[16]

This succession of disasters, natural and human, brought all deep mining in the Tombstone district to a halt. More than two-thirds of the town's population drifted off to other mining fields, while Contention City joined Charleston in the category of ghost town; the post office, the last symbol of life, was closed on November 26, 1888. And Galeyville likewise became a memory. In 1888 the San Simon Cattle Company either drove out or bought out the few remaining residents, most of them squatters on abandoned property; the little that remained in 1888, having escaped a fire that had devastated the town, was carried away to be used in constructing houses in the town of Paradise (scene of a brief mining flurry in 1901 when a vein of ore was discovered there). Tombstone seemed destined to suffer the same fate as the nearby towns, although sufficient people still lived there in 1889 to ensure it some sort of success; it continued to exist mainly because it was the county seat and thus had a small payroll every month, and because the ranchers in the area needed a town in which to trade. J. Rowland Hill, who visited Tombstone in 1889 commented about the disasters and the quarrels between mine owners, "All these counter-influences have been against the growth of the city; and for four years this partial paralysis has to some extent crippled the energies of the citizens."[17]

Nor was the water problem to be solved in the near future. The various mining corporations with holdings in the district became engaged in a waiting game, each trying to hold out until some other company grew impatient. All knew that valuable ores were beneath the water level, just as all knew that the first company to pump out its own shafts would also pump the water out of all the other shafts. Thus it would be more profitable to let some other company erect the needed pumping machinery than to rush in first. J. Rowland Hill was so angered at this situation in Tombstone during his visit of 1889 that he wrote, "It reminds me of the design used by many banking institutions in which a watch dog is represented as lying at the door of the money-vault. He does not molest the safe or its contents, nor allow others to do it; he can not handle the key, while these wealthy mine owners do hold the key to the situation, and by a single turn can liberate millions, and start the wheel of prosperity."[18]

But prosperity was not just around the corner. Nor was it for any of the other silver-producing areas of the American West; the truth was there was too much silver, and the price kept tumbling. The Bland-Allison Act of 1878 with its provision to purchase $2,000,000 to $4,000,000 in bullion each month had not kept the price near $1.29 an ounce as had been hoped. By 1890 the price was at so disastrous a level that silver production was not paying rich dividends. Thus congressional representatives of the silver states were looking that year to secure passage of federal legislation that would raise the price artificially. Fortunately the political situation made this possible. Representatives of the farm states also were seeking legislation which would lead to some inflation of the currency and thereby bring relief to their constituents, many of whom were bankrupt because of the increasing value of the "hard" money of the day. And in 1890 congressional representatives of the manufacturing interests wanted to raise the tariff. The result was a swapping of votes that saw both the McKinley Tariff passed (providing for a general upward trend in import duties) and the Sherman Silver Purchase Act securing final approval. The latter provided for the issuance of federal "legal tender notes" (or money) sufficient in amount to pay for 4,500,000 ounces of silver bullion each month at the prevailing market price. This act would be repealed on November 1, 1893, by which time the government had bought 169,000,000 ounces of silver at a cost of approximately $156,000,000—or an average of slightly more than ninety-two cents per ounce. This was far below the good years of $1.29 per ounce and not enough to cause a renewed boom in silver mining as advocates of the measure had intended.

Yet passage of the Sherman Silver Purchase Act in the summer of 1890 did spur some of the companies to install pumping machinery. However, they quickly learned that the expense involved was greater than the value of the silver they were extracting. Moreover, nothing could be done to solve the dilemma unless ore bodies of far higher silver content were found, which were not, or unless all the companies joined together to share the cost equally and thus lower the expenses of each individual company—and that proved difficult, if not impossible to achieve. Thus Tombstone continued to wane during the 1890s. More and more miners became so discouraged that they moved south to work for the copper companies at Bisbee and Douglas or north to Globe, Miami, Clifton, and Morenci. Houses in Tombstone gradually were abandoned, sinking into ruin as ever-waiting nature reclaimed Goose Flats. A few small ore bodies above the water line continued to be worked, even after deep mining was suspended, but the continually declining price of silver discouraged even those pitiful efforts. The smokestacks of the stamp mills gradually stopped belching forth the smoke that signaled prosperity.

Fortunately at this time in Cochise County, the grass was still growing. Thus ranching produced some income for southern Arizona even as the mines closed. And there were some colorful cattlemen who came to the vicinity, men who in their own way showed the same tenacity and perseverance as had Ed Schieffelin. For example, one of the most famous of these early cattlemen was Henry Clay Hooker, a refugee from the California gold rush. He had raised his capital to begin his cattle operations by purchasing 500 turkeys in California at $1.50 apiece, driving them overland to the Nevada mining camps, and selling them for $5.00 a head. Then in 1867 he secured a contract to supply beef to army posts in northern Arizona, buying the cattle in Texas and Arizona and trail-driving them to their destination. Finally in 1872 he established his Sierra Bonita Ranch in Sulphur Springs Valley, and there, despite the incursions of the Chiricahua Apaches—which included one dramatic face-to-face meeting between Hooker and Cochise—he persisted in his operation. Within a few years he had the largest and most successful ranch in the territory. He introduced the new breeds of cattle—shorthorns, Durhams, and Herefords—to the 800 square miles that he controlled. And for the comfort of the guests who visited his empire, he kept a dairy herd, flocks of poultry, and a large garden. He also pioneered in breeding and racing horses noted for their stamina and beauty.

Contributing to the increase in cattle ranching in southeastern Arizona was the final victory over the Chiricahua and Warm Springs Apaches, whose land it originally had been. They had fled San Carlos in September 1881, but General George Crook, who returned to command the department in 1882, had pursued them relentlessly in Mexico and had persuaded them by negotiation to return to their reservation in January 1884. The same unhappy conditions pertained at San Carlos, however, and in May 1885 Nachez, Geronimo, and some 140 renegades broke for Sonora again. The campaign that followed was marked by attacks on Crook's Indian scouts by Mexican scalp bounty hunters, international tensions, and occasional raids into Arizona; but in March 1886 Crook met with the hostiles just south of the international boundary and secured a surrender. As the renegades were on their way north, however, a wandering whiskey peddler sold them whiskey, and Geronimo, Nachez, eighteen warriors, and nineteen women and children again fled into Sonora. General Crook was forced into resigning in the furor that followed, and General Nelson A. Miles came to Arizona to force the Apaches into unconditional surrender. When his plan of relentless pursuit failed to force his goal, he likewise turned to a policy of negotiation. Using Lieutenant Charles B. Gatewood as his instrument, he arranged a surrender conference in southeastern Arizona on September 3-4, 1886, at which he promised the Apaches they would be imprisoned in Florida for two years and then returned to Arizona. That promise was broken even as the renegades were on their way to Florida—they would be held as prisoners of war until 1913 and would return west only as far as Fort Sill, Oklahoma.[19]

Their removal meant total American ownership of southeastern Arizona—and safety for the cattlemen. Thus in that vicinity grew many ranches in addition to the pioneering effort of Henry Clay Hooker. The Empire Ranch was established in 1876 by Walter L. Vail and his English partners, H. R. Hislop and John Harvey; located in the Santa Rita Mountains, it proved very successful. Other operations in the vicinity included the San Simon Cattle Company and the Tombstone Land and Cattle Company; the latter was incorporated with $100,000 capitalization in 1887 to "purchase and sell land for cattle ranges and water rights as well as to raise and market cattle." Its owners were John Volz, Peter Volz, Joseph Pascholy, Ernst Stom, F. A. Abbott, and Adam Bing.[20]

And it was one of these ranchers who finally "tamed" the cowboy element of Tombstone and Cochise County: John Horton Slaughter, born in 1841 in the Republic of Texas, the child of frontier parents. He had grown to manhood in the era of cattle baronies in West Texas, and his relatives would establish one of the family dynasties of Texas ranchers. For him, however, the far West held a lure that could not be resisted, and he arrived in the San Pedro Valley in 1879, the same year that Tombstone was aborning. Mining was not for him, although he could not as yet afford the ranch he wanted; instead for several years he worked as a contractor and wholesaler of beef, going as far afield as Oregon before determining to cast his future with southeastern Arizona. The site he chose was the famous San Bernardino grant totaling approximately 65,000 acres and dating from a grant by the Mexican government in 1822 to Lieutenant Ignacio Perez. Most of this land was inside Mexico, as was the title; Slaughter purchased it from the owner, G. Andrade of Guaymas, Sonora. Living first in an adobe structure located near the old Perez hacienda, Slaughter soon was running cattle on both sides of the international line; and he dammed the springs and constructed a network of irrigation canals so that eventually he had thirty families living on the ranch to harvest hay,

John H. Slaughter, the sheriff who rid Cochise County of the outlaws.
Courtesy Arizona Historical Society.

fruit, and vegetables, along with a score and more of cowboys to herd his cattle.

In 1886 Slaughter formed a partnership with George W. Lang, a famous trail driver who owned the Bato Pico Ranch on the Bavispe River in Sonora. The Bato Pico adjoined the San Bernardino on the south, and the two partners thereafter purchased cattle in Sonora, held them for fattening on the San Bernardino, and then marketed the animals in California. They even operated a slaughter house in Los Angeles for much of this beef. In 1890, however, Slaughter bought the Bato Pico from Lang, along with all its cattle, and the partnership was dissolved. Meanwhile, he had made a reputation in a different line of endeavor, for in the election of November 1886 he was chosen the third sheriff of Cochise County, his job was to end the cowboy menace concentrated in Galeyville.

Actually Slaughter had encountered less trouble from the Galeyville element in the years 1879-86 than he had from Tombstone. Galeyville was the headquarters of the cowboy element almost from the moment of its birth in November 1880. Curly Bill Brocius was the acknowledged "boss" of the town, and in the nearby gorges and canyons he and his men held stolen cattle for shipment north or south. When they were occasionally caught and brought to trial in the county courthouse in Tombstone, these rustlers would employ silver-tongued lawyers such as Marcus A. Smith (later one of Arizona's first United States senators) or Al English, spellbinders who worked magic on juries—when a large number of murderous cronies sat in the courtroom audience and by their presence did not persuade the twelve men to vote for acquittal of the accused.

John Slaughter had walked the middle ground through the wars of the first half of the 1880s. He took no part in the arrests and trials of the cowboys and the Earps, yet neither did he tolerate thefts from his own herds. His fights were private, his courage well known, and his gun deadly. Thus he survived and prospered. Then in the fall of 1886 his fellow citizens began looking for a tough, honest man to run for sheriff on the Democratic ticket in Cochise County. Bob Hatch, who had succeeded John Behan to the position of sheriff, was competent enough, but he had made little headway in ending the cowboy menace. Slaughter campaigned only in an indifferent manner, but the voters wanted him and thus he was inaugurated as sheriff early in 1887.

The former Texas Ranger took the initiative, not waiting for the cowboy faction to make the first move. Some men he told to leave the area—and they did; others fought, only to die or be brought to trial. Some of them were convicted, to be shipped to the Territorial Prison at Yuma, the infamous "Hell Hole" where John Behan now presided as warden. Some of the men Slaughter arrested were freed by juries only to be threatened by the vigilantes. Sheriff Slaughter would have none of that and faced down the occasional mobs. Often his life was endangered, but his good planning—along with a much-vaunted intuition—enabled him to survive. He was re-elected in 1888 and served a second term, aided by agents of the territorial cattleman's association (which had been established in 1884 and which finally was becoming effective) in his fights with the rustlers. And when Slaughter retired from office by choice in 1890, it was with the knowledge that Cochise County largely was as law-abiding and safe as any other part of the United States. He had done his duty at a considerable financial sacrifice, neglecting his ranch holdings to pursue criminals; he had put no notches on his six-shooter, he never bragged about the men he had to kill, and he never shot unless forced to do so. And his successor, Tombstone photographer C. S. Fly, recognized Slaughter's contributions to the county by naming him in January 1895 a deputy sheriff, a position of honor Slaughter would hold until his death in 1922.[21]

The year when Slaughter retired from office, 1890, there no longer was any real attraction for robbers in Tombstone and vicinity. The town was sinking into oblivion, the days of large bullion shipments and big payrolls a forgotten dream. One by one businesses failed, and the rival newspapers gradually succumbed to brankruptcy or else merged until only the *Epitaph* was left—and it only a weekly surviving by printing the county's legal notices. No mining was taking place at deep levels where the rich ore was located, and there was little activity at more shallow depths. By 1901 fewer than 1000 people were in the town. Meanwhile copper was steadily growing as the major source of mining revenue for the territory as the electrical revolution swept the United States; in 1888 Arizona's output of the red metal was valued at $5,000,000, a figure that grew annually; by 1910 its value was $37,800,000. But there was little romance in copper, and men still dreamed of tapping the silver wealth that lay underwater in Tombstone's mines.

This dream periodically led to bursts of optimism in the columns of the *Epitaph*. In February 1900 the editor was moved to comment, "The darkest hours of the night are those which immediately precede the dawn. We believe the time is not far distant when our grand old camp will rise from the waves and shake her crested head aloft with pride as of yore."[22] His metaphors were mixed, but his hopes were not.

More practical men likewise were thinking the same thoughts, and this led at the turn of the twentieth century to the organization of the Development Company of America, the brainchild of E. B. Gage, a noted mining engineer, and Frank M. Murphy, an optimist who dreamed of emulating Adolph Sutro's Nevada tunnel and draining the mining district at Tombstone. Murphy was a brother of Nathan Oakes Murphy, twice territorial governor of Arizona (1892-93 and 1898-1902). Frank Murphy thus had good political connections for his scheme, and he had the financial experience to undertake the effort; it was he who had organized the Prescott and Phoenix Railroad, a spur line to connect the Santa Fe with the territorial capital and join with the Southern Pacific at Maricopa Wells. This short line, completed in 1895, had proved a success, and it gave Murphy access to financiers in the East. And Gage, the owner and manager of the Grand Central Company, gave them access to the mining properties of the district.

In October 1900 the two men visited Tombstone in company with F. M. Staunton, the former superintendent of the Tough Nut Mine and at the time of the visit the superintendent of the Congress Mine. A study of the situation led Murphy to propose the

Frank Murphy, who formed the consolidated mining concern to pump
the water out of the mines, thereby reviving Tombstone from 1901 to
1911. *Courtesy Arizona Historical Society.*

opening of a master drainage shaft, one large enough to draw off
all the water; he then would install steam-driven force pumps of
sufficient size at the head of this shaft to pump out the entire district. And as the water was lowered, he would drill the master shaft
yet deeper, the pumps would be moved down to the new level, and
yet more water would be pumped out. This leap-frogging process
could continue downward, said Murphy, until a projected maximum depth of 1000 feet was attained. The editor of the *Epitaph*
was so encouraged that on October 21 he wrote, "A party of distinguished arrivals were in Tombstone today, and their presence
gave rise to the general hope that the dark murky clouds that have
long hovered over Tombstone's industrial atmosphere would rise
and reveal a luminous silver lining." Warming to his task, the editor continued, "Whispers, murmurs and rumors of the opening of
the Tombstone mines under a consolidated management, would,
if consummated, bring about a dawn of prosperity never equalled
hereabouts, and the sunshine of consequent good times would start
the sluggish commercial blood into the renewed activity and vigor
of halcyon days."

In September 1901 E. B. Gage returned, ready to put the plan
into operation. The Development Company of America had at last
formed a subsidiary concern, the Tombstone Consolidated Mines
Company, whose purpose was to bring out the ore as fast as the
water was pumped out. The company booklet for 1902 would state
that this concern had accomplished the long-sought consolidation
of the various mines around Tombstone; it had secured title to
more than seventy claims, including all the major ones, and controlled approximately two square miles. The list that followed
proved the truth of the assertion, for on it were the Contention,
the Grand Central, and the old Tombstone Mill and Mining Company's eighteen claims, along with all the mills, millsites, buildings,
and machinery.[23] Apparently the El Paso and Southwestern Railroad was impressed with this scheme, for in 1901 it began building
a spur to the town of Tombstone, to reach there the following year
and thus provide it with the rail service it had sought for so long.

Gage's return in September 1901 and the first work at sinking the major shaft of draining led the *Epitaph* editor on September 18 to exult: "The mines again will be in operation. Prosperity has superseded depression. The steam whistles awaken the slumberer, darkening smokes waft lazily over the erstwhile dreamy city casting upon the earth portentious shadows of future prosperity—a silhouette of the past—there are no laggards here." By November 1902 the pumps were installed at the 600-foot level and the shaft was down another 40 feet; the pumps had been taken from the Contention, rebuilt, and reinstalled, their capacity some 2,500,000 gallons every twenty-four hours.[24] Two more pumps arrived, both made by Prescott, both of the duplex, triple expansion condensing type, both capable of raising 1500 gallons per minute.[25] By the end of 1903 work had passed the 700-foot level and was proceeding smoothly. Ore was coming out at the rate of two carloads per day.

By 1905 the project of the Consolidated Mines, as the concern was called locally, was showing success. The main shaft measured 7 feet by 22 feet and had four compartments, two for hoisting and two for pumping. A substantial double engine flat-cable hoist was in place, along with a steel headframe 79 feet high and 30 feet wide. The pumping plant in totality weighed more than a million pounds and was an imposing sight. Moreover, the operation was working. At the 800-foot level the pumps were raising 2,300,000 gallons of water each day, while the cross-cuts that opened off it were being worked for ore of good quality. At the surface this ore was being reduced to bulk concentrate and then shipped, two and three carloads daily, to El Paso, Texas. Project Director Murphy even began reworking the low-grade ore and the waste dumps from the earlier period—at a profit thanks to new methods of extracting the silver that had been developed in the last two decades. And fortunately the world price of silver jumped just as the Development Company of America got its operations under way on a large scale, so that for the next few years the company showed a respectable profit on its investment. Production was averaging half a million dollars annually.[26]

By the time the company reached the 1000-foot level, additional pumps had been ordered for installation. These were placed in operation in June of 1908. A total of 10,000,000 gallons could be pumped every twenty-four hours, although the average was still below 7,000,000 gallons daily. But again it was the declining price of silver that hurt Tombstone's chances for an economic recovery. The price had fallen to 47¢ an ounce in 1902 for a historic low, then had risen to 71¢ in 1906, and in 1907 fluctuated between 70¢ and 54¢ an ounce. The final issue of the *Epitaph* for 1908, published on December 31, showed no failure of hope: "And so at the passing of that old year, Tombstone, DEAR Old Tombstone, takes on new heart and courage and turns her eyes to where is breaking the dawn of a greater prosperity than she ever enjoyed before. . . . The assurance is almost positive that before 1909 shall have spun its circle Tombstone will be hailed as it once was, the greatest mining camp of the west."

The dawn which the editor had been predicting for so long never arrived. In fact, permanent night settled on the town that year of 1909. The exact reasons for the work stopping at the Consolidated Mines perhaps never will be known. Frank Murphy announced that the fuel supply for the pumps at the 1000-foot level had been defective; a tank car thought to be bringing fuel oil had delivered salt water instead. The pump quit, and water began quietly moving upward, thereby drowning the future of Tombstone. When it reached the 900-foot level, the overloaded pumps at higher levels gave out. Murphy then announced that the drainage system was ruined.

Yet Murphy's argument seems specious. Repairs could have been made on the boiler of the pump at the 1000-foot level with sufficient speed to prevent the flooding; moreover, a temporary flooding would not have damaged the cross-cuts and drifts cut away from the main shaft. But Murphy was through with Tombstone, probably because of the falling price of silver—and possibly because the rich ore was almost exhausted. Just before Christmas of 1910 the *Epitaph* noted that the Consolidated Mines Company had filed notice of an amendment to its articles of incorporation that would allow it to borrow $6,000,000; then in January 1911 the paper hinted that the company was in financial difficulty. It was, and again gloom descended on Tombstone as mining activity ceased. Phelps Dodge Corporation, the copper-mining giant of southern Arizona, began quietly purchasing the claims in the Tombstone district, claims which today are still in private ownership—and unused—while arguments continue apace about the quality of the ore under the water.

The estimates of the total value of gold and silver mined at Tombstone have been varied. The most believable figure is approximately $80,000,000, the bulk of this in the period 1878-86—and thus at a time when Arizona desperately needed an economic lift. The silver had brought thousands of miners to the region and had persuaded the Southern Pacific to lay its tracks through the area. Further, the miners had attracted ranchers and farmers to the vicinity; they remained after the mines closed and constituted a permanent population. And even after the mines had begun to flood, the workers there provided a source of skilled labor for the emerging copper industry. Tombstone's significance thus did not lay in the violent outlaws which it had attracted. Rather it should be remembered for its economic impact at a time of relative depression.

Yet the little town that had sprung into existence on Goose Flats did not vanish after the Consolidated Mines Company folded. It was a county seat and a merchandise point for a few ranchers. And there were a few hardy souls living in it who believed that somehow someday it would be reborn; a vigorous city would arise, not like a phoenix bird from its ashes but rather like a submarine out of the water beneath the ground—for these optimists still believed that rich ore was underground and underwater if only the price of silver would rise to the point of making it profitable to recover it. Such dreams die very slowly—and just as slowly as the dream died with the passing of old-timers so the town was dying. What Tombstone badly needed was a new source of revenue, along with a new reason for existence. In 1929 it found that source and that reason, thus earning the self-bestowed title "The Town Too Tough to Die."

The Last Bonanza

Most cities of the Western United States, after they had achieved a certain maturity, not only turned their backs on their frontier beginnings but also deliberately tried to hide the crudities of their birth. They downplayed the violence and the raw conditions associated with their beginnings and stressed cultural heritage of the past. Descendants of the pioneers transformed their ancestors into gentlemen, ladies, and philanthropists; they created historical societies whose function it was to launder history and make it presentable.

But not Tombstone. As the town sank back into a slow decline toward oblivion after the mines finally closed about 1910, the remaining old-timers had their memories—and that was all. And those memories were kept green by a constant retelling of the days of glory. In fact, the memories, like good wine, seemed to improve with age. The human characteristics of the founders of Tombstone became virtues in reverse. Mediocre characters were made into lawless tigers; bad men became heroes in an environment dedicated to preserving the most colorful aspects of the past; the shady ladies became angels of mercy. It seemed that the town's remaining population rejoiced in what other cities tried to hide.

And as the business activity of the town moved ever slower, there was more time for talk, for remembering, for reminiscing. Of course, much of this talk centered on the subsequent careers of the three discoverers of the Tombstone silver deposits: the Schieffelins and Dick Gird. Of these three, the first to die was Al Schieffelin, who succumbed to tuberculosis at a young age and did not live to enjoy his wealth. Ed Schieffelin meanwhile had resumed the life of a prospector. He listed his permanent address as that of his mother in Alameda, California, but he stayed there only between trips to distant mountains. Even marriage in San Francisco did not still his restless wanderings which led him as far afield as Alaska. Death caught him on May 14, 1896, in Oregon; he died at the doorway of his cabin, located twenty miles east of Canyonville. The restless spirit was on him, even at the last; to a friend he had written, "I am getting restless here in Oregon and wish to go somewhere that has wealth, for the digging of it. . . . I like the excitement of being right up against the earth, trying to coax her gold away and scatter it."[1]

When his body was discovered, there was some thought of foul play but an intensive investigation ruled that out, as it did suicide. On his body were found money, his watch, some business papers, and a set of plans for the immediate future that included another prospect. Nearby was a small sack of ore which, when assayed, proved to be worth $2000 to the ton. Perhaps Schieffelin died happy, believing he had found yet another bonanza. His will stipulated that all his property go to his wife with the exception of $15,000 in University of Arizona bonds; these he left to a brother (he had no children).

Schieffelin once was heard to remark that the two most glorious nights of his life had been those when he had slept at the side of his initial discovery in the San Pedro Valley. His will reflected this memory:

> It is my wish, if convenient, to be buried in the dress of a prospector, my old pick and canteen with me, on top of the granite hills about three miles westerly from the City of Tombstone, Ari-

zona, and that a monument such as prospectors build when locating a mining claim be built over my grave, and no other slab or monument erected. And I request that none of my friends wear crape. Under no circumstances do I want to be buried in a graveyard or cemetery.[2]

His brother Charles made known his wish to the citizens of Tombstone in a telegram dated May 17, 1897, and Ed's wishes were respected. On May 23 his body was interred at the site he had selected, the old location of the brief town of Watervale. His wife, mother, and brother were present for a moving funeral that included a eulogy by Colonel William Herring. And the monument erected at the spot was in the shape of a miner's location notice—but on a slab twenty-feet square and grounded on solid granite. The inscription was simple: "Ed Schieffelin, died May 12, 1897, aged 49 years and 8 months. A dutiful son, a faithful husband, a kind brother, a true friend."

Dick Gird, the third of the triumvirate that discovered Tombstone, had gone on to an even more distinguished career than either of the other two men. At his Chino Ranch he first began trying to improve the quality of the livestock, importing fine stallions from France along with pureblood Holstein cattle which he cross-bred with Durhams. Then for a time he experimented with silk-worm culture, but eventually he discovered that the future—at least his future on the ranch—was in sugar beets. His experiments with them, lasting four years, showed that they would grow well in that part of California. This effort to encourage their growth coincided with land speculation then rampant in southern California, and in 1887 he subdivided 23,000 acres of his ranch into ten-acre parcels. To encourage buyers, he laid out the city of Chino and connected it with the nearby city of Ontario by means of a narrow-gauge railroad which he constructed at his own expense. In order to supply the settlers to whom he sold land with a market for the sugar beets he encouraged them to grow, he put up the land and the money with which the Oxnard brothers constructed the Chino Beet Sugar Factory (which later would become part of the American Beet Sugar Company).

Also, Gird continued experimenting to improve the beet sugar industry. In this quest he made use of the first steam plow in southern California, and he designed seeders, cultivators, and other tools to be used by the 600 men he employed after his land sales proved disappointing. For the children of the people who did purchase his ten-acre plots, he helped create the school district in Chino in 1888, personally donating the land and the building and paying the salary for the teacher of the first class.

Then in 1885 he became involved in yet another venture of startling magnitude. With several capitalists as partners, he helped establish the California-Mexico Land and Cattle Company; he and the others subscribed money to purchase half a million acres of land in Mexico on which cattle were raised for shipment northward for fattening in California—on beet by-products. Then the animals were marketed. The venture proved very profitable, for the partners were wise enough to put the Mexican commander of troops in the vicinity of their land in Mexico on their payroll; this prevented their Sonoran employees from stealing. In 1901 this land was sold to the Cananea Consolidated Copper Company of the fabulous Colonel William Greene, again at a substantial profit for the investors.

One other curious note about Gird's life came to light while he was in California. Prior to his move to Arizona in the 1860s, he had been friends with John Bidwell, a Forty-niner-turned-farmer who pioneered the introduction of fruit and nut trees in California. Reportedly the two men had even done some prospecting together. And in 1886 Bidwell's heirs sued Gird in the California courts, claiming that half of what Gird had received from his Tombstone venture rightfully belonged to them inasmuch as Bidwell and Gird had been partners at the time. The heirs lost this suit when it finally came to trial, but they appealed the verdict—whereupon Gird settled out of court with them for a reported $100,000. He died in southern California on May 30, 1910.[3]

Death would eventually claim all the major participants in Tombstone's days of glory. John Vosburg would live to January 1931, dying at Los Angeles at the age of ninety. Slightly more than a year later in the same city, John P. Clum died after having a second and even third career, but not involved with journalism. When he departed Tombstone for the more effete and sedate East, he joined the Chief Post Office Inspector's Office in Washington, D. C. Then in January 1885 he returned to Tombstone, having been appointed postmaster, and then served as city auditor. However, he saw that the town was dying, and late in 1886 he resigned his city offices and connections and moved to San Bernardino, California. There he dabbled in real estate brokerage, managed the San Bernardino County Citrus Fair, and worked briefly on the *Los Angeles Examiner* as an assistant editor.

Then in 1891 he returned to Washington to spend the next twenty years with the Office of Post Office Inspector. This service would bring him years of adventure in all parts of the United States, even to Alaska in 1898 to organize the postal service there and in the Aleutian Islands; on that trip he and his nineteen-year-old son Woodworth traveled more than 10,000 miles. Two years later he returned to Alaska, as he would every summer for the next five years, to check on the postal service. And on one of these trips he met an old crony from his Tombstone days, Wyatt Earp.

In April 1910 he retired from the postal service, whereupon he took to the lecture circuit as a self-styled "Trail-Blazer of Civilization." His background in amateur theatricals, in which he had participated in Tombstone as well as in Tucson, Washington, and even Fairbanks, Alaska, made him successful on the lecture circuit —that and the fact that they were free to the public courtesy of the Southern Pacific Railroad. After several other assorted ventures, Clum retired to Los Angeles to write of his adventures; and several articles bearing his by-line were published (to be used by his son Woodworth in the semi-autobiographical story of Clum's life, *Apache Agent*, which appeared in 1936). He died in Los Angeles on May 2, 1932, at the age of eighty-one.[4]

The members of the old dangerous gang, both city and country, which had plagued Tombstone and which had given it a national image of violence, likewise went to various rewards. Doc Holliday died of tuberculosis in a Colorado sanatorium in 1887, probably at age thirty-five. Buckskin Frank Leslie remained in the vicinity of Tombstone until 1890 when he was convicted of the murder of Molly Bradshaw; he served seven years before receiving a pardon and wandering into Sonora and then to Alaska, reportedly dying in San Francisco in 1925 when in his eighties.

And Wyatt Earp, who fled Arizona under indictment for murder, likewise spent time in Alaska. From Arizona he had gone to San Francisco. There he met Josephine Sarah Marcus, daughter of a wealthy merchant, and the two of them began living together. In 1883 Earp was in Denver, followed by travel in Kansas, Wyoming, Idaho, and Texas. Then in 1886 they settled in San Diego for four years while Earp operated a saloon, then moved in 1890 to San Francisco where he publicized himself and raced horses. Next he was in Nome operating a saloon during the gold rush to Alaska; after four years at that location, he turned up in the boom town of Tonopah, Nevada, also to operate a saloon, as he did later at Goldfield, Nevada, in 1905. Finally in 1906 he settled at Los Angeles, where he lived during his last years. And, according to newspaper accounts, he occasionaly tried a swindle; but mainly he was seeking publicity. He tried to interest William S. Hart, a movie cowboy, in the story of his life; that failing, he spoke with writer Walter Noble Burns, and he had several interviews with Stuart N. Lake, a journalist. Before anything could come of these efforts, however, Earp died on January 3, 1929, at the age of eighty. Just before then he had posed for one last photograph, one which his wife said had made him look like a banker. Honorary pallbearers at his funeral at Colma, a town near San Francisco, included John Clum and George Parsons. And even in his death there was some notoriety; thieves stole the 300-pound grave marker erected over Earp.[5]

Two years after Wyatt Earp died, he finally received the pub-

Marcus A. Smith, Tombstone lawyer who often represented Arizona in Congress. *Courtesy Arizona Historical Society.*

licity he had sought for so long. Stuart Lake that year published *Wyatt Earp: Frontier Marshal*, a distorted, hell-for-leather epic which placed the dead gunman in the tradition of Robin Hood and Sir Galahad; he was transformed into a man of total good fighting against total evil in Tombstone.[6] And since that pioneering effort a half-dozen biographies have appeared that assert a basis in fact, along with several dozen others with few pretensions of accuracy. The full truth will not become public knowledge in the foreseeable future, for much of the evidence about Earp's life has fallen into the hands of self-advertised collectors, men who all too often have made a cult of secrecy of their holdings.

Yet in Tombstone there was no effort at secrecy in talking about the old days. In those years following the closing of the mines in 1911, the city was growing anemic but the legends were improving with age. The heroes and villains of the old-timers' stories—the Earps, the Clantons, the McLowry's, Clum, and the rest—had moved away or else died, and thus there was no one in Tombstone to contradict the accounts and anecdotes which were told and re-told—embellishments growing like desert flowers after a rain each time they were recounted.

"Remember Rotten Row?" someone would ask, and it would evoke a dozen stories about the lawyers of the good old days. Rotten Row had been a portion of Fourth Street (between Tough Nut and Allen streets) inhabited by members of Tombstone's legal fraternity. One of the favorite heroes of such stories was Marcus Aurelius Smith, ever popular because he represented Arizona in the United States Senate from 1912 to 1920. In those early days he was newly arrived from his native Kentucky, a young politician who frequently represented the territory in congress (a territory was allotted one non-voting delegate). He drank with the boys when he was in town, and he gambled—how he loved to gamble, especially at faro. The story most often told about Smith involved a certain day when slightly drunk he set out to find a faro game. At the Crystal Palace the only games of chance under way were blackjack and poker. At the Oriental he had no better luck. Then at the

Pony Saloon he chanced upon two transients playing faro, but obviously with a crooked box. Nevertheless he sat in.

Word spread that good old Mark Smith was being taken, and some of his friends grew so concerned they approached him. "Come out of it," they told Smith. "Don't you know they're dealing the best of it? You haven't got a chance to win."

Smith was not the least concerned. "What of it?" he replied. "It's the only game in town, ain't it?"[7]

And there was Smith's partner, Allen R. English, who came to Tombstone in 1880 at the age of twenty to muck in the mines and then read law until he passed the bar exam. By 1887 he was district attorney, an office he would hold twice more. But the people loved him for his alcoholic humor, while his clients appreciated his way with a jury. Once when a judge fined him $25 for contempt of court for being drunk, English delighted the whole town with his reply: "Your honor, $25 wouldn't pay for half the contempt I have for this court."[8]

On another occasion English, while under consideration in Washington for an appointment as district attorney for the territory of Arizona, was discussing the festivities that would accompany San Juan's Day (June 24). According to local legend still prevalent in southern Arizona, it always rained on San Juan's Day, as one of the men speaking with English forecast. "By God, this is one San Juan's Day it won't rain," English told them.

One man in the crowd offered a bet that it would. "I'll take that bet," declared English, then added, "and if it rains, I'll strip off naked and stand under that water spout." He pointed to a drain pike at the corner of the building housing Billy King's Saloon. San Juan's Day dawned cloudy and dark, and soon the water was coming down. True to his word, Allen strolled stark naked out of King's Saloon to the water spout and stood under it. Not long afterward he learned that he would not receive the appointment as district attorney for the territory. When he inquired of friends why the appointment would not be made, he was informed that a picture of him standing naked under the drain spout had been sent anony-

Al English, Tombstone lawyer and colorful figure. *Courtesy Arizona Historical Society.*

Nosie Kate, noted madame in Tombstone. *Courtesy Arizona Historical Society.*

mously to the nation's capital with an inscription stating, "This is the man you are considering for U. S. District Attorney." Everyone suspected the picture had been taken and mailed by a Mrs. Warnekros, the owner of the Arlington Rooming House in Tombstone and an opponent of drinking and high living.[9]

And the Tenderloin District. Remember the girls there in that section of town on the north side of Sixth Street reserved for them? They came out to shop, they ate in the Can Can Restaurant, they rented carriages and rode through town. Talk—and rarely would someone claim to be speaking from first-hand experience on this subject—would lead to mention of such ladies as Blonde Marie, a French woman whose house on Sixth Street was managed with quiet efficiency; her frame house was different in that she had only French girls and she did not have a bar. In the mid-1890s she returned to Paris a rich woman.

And there was Kate Lowe, remembered in Tombstone by her nickname, Nosey Kate. Like the Earps, she was a refugee from Dodge City, arriving in 1879 to purchase a tent in which she opened a "dance hall" and bar. Nosey Kate's place was at the very bottom of Tombstone's social life, but it suited the rough taste of the Cornish miners, whose idea of culture was to get very drunk and then bed down one of the girls. Kate soon made enough money to invest in a frame shack in the "district," and in this she sold "soldier whiskey," took money for the dancing, and received a cut from the prostituting. Then in 1881 she went too far, for one evening she decided to roll a buyer for the Miller and Lux Ranch of California. After pouring large amounts of her raw whiskey down his throat, Kate slipped him the knockout drops; but still he fought back when she tried to lift his large roll, whereupon she cracked his skull with a heavy beer bottle. Thinking he was dead, she had the body dumped outside town—only to see it walk in an hour later with the law and shouting that it had been robbed. Kate managed an escape, never to be seen in Tombstone again. Her house fell to Emmy Blair who operated it in the same liberal fashion.[10]

And the Chinese. Who could forget China Mary? In its heyday

Nellie Cashman, who operated a restaurant in Tombstone and was noted for her acts of charity to miners. *Courtesy Arizona Historical Society.*

Tombstone boasted an Oriental colony of 400 to 500. They did the laundry and housekeeping along with most of the cooking. And when someone wanted a houseboy, he went to China Mary, the leader of the Chinese community; she provided the needed help and even guaranteed that the servants she sent would not steal. In addition to this employment service, Mary sold cheese, Chinese foodstuff, and knicknacks which she imported—along with opium to be used in Chinese opium dens and also by a few of the prostitutes who were hooked on it. But Mary was best remembered for her generosity. A miner down on his luck could usually get a loan from her, while those in genuine need often received money as a gift. She also would take the sick and injured into her home, at least those she liked, and nurse them back to health.[11]

And there was Nellie Cashman. Aunt Nell they called her. Nellie Cashman, born in Queenstown, Ireland, came to the United States with a sister. Arriving in San Francisco in 1869, Nellie saw her sister married and then moved to Tucson where she established Delmonico's Restaurant, advertising "the best meal in town." When Tombstone boomed, she moved there to start the Russ House, also a restaurant featuring "the best meal in town." Still not thirty years of age, she never had scandal associated with her name; in fact, she became known as an angel of mercy. She had living with her in Tombstone her widowed sister and the five children from that marriage; and when her sister died in 1883, she raised the five orphans as if they were her own. In addition to this, Nellie was always available when someone was needed to help the sick or the injured. She became a one-woman director of charities, and few could refuse her pleas for donations to aid this or that worthy cause.

And in 1884 when the sheriff was preparing to hang the five men convicted of the Bisbee massacre, Nellie took it upon herself to worry about the souls of the five men awaiting execution. A Catholic herself, she volunteered as confessor when no priest was found available for two of the prisoners who were of that faith; and so sincere was her manner that the other three condemned men converted and allowed her to hear their confessions. As this was transpiring, the five men heard the sound of hammers and realized that their execution was to be made into a sideshow. Witnesses could get into the courtyard only by invitation, but hundreds more wanted to watch. An enterprising man who owned the adjacent land was building a grandstand high enough to enable people to see over the wall, intending to sell seats for the spectacle. The sheriff would not prevent this, for it would cost him votes. Nellie went out quietly and found a few rugged miners to aid her; meeting at two in the morning, they reduced the grandstand to kindling —and it could not be rebuilt in time for its owner to sell tickets to, the execution. Nellie was another of Tombstone's pioneers who made the rush to the Klondike; she died at Victoria, British Columbia, on January 4, 1925.[12]

Yes, Tombstone had a host of memories, but that was cold comfort to a town that was dying—would, in fact, have long since joined Charleston and Contention and Galeyville as a ghost town but for the jobs provided by its status as the county seat and the supplies purchased by ranchers. Then in 1928 one of the old-timers, former deputy sheriff Billy Breakenridge, published *Helldorado* and received national attention thereby. Perhaps, thought some of the residents, they might open a new vein of ore: the tourist. In October 1929 they staged a celebration which they named after the book of reminiscences, Helldorado Week. It was scheduled to take place during the week wherein October 26 fell, as that was the date of the famed gunfight at the OK Corral. And the year 1929 seemed a legitimate one to begin the celebration, for it was the fiftieth anniversary of the founding of the town.

All pioneers of Tombstone's early years who were still alive were invited guests at the celebration, which featured reenactments of hangings and killings, of shootouts in the streets, of battles with Indians, and of the antics of naughty ladies and the theater. John Clum journeyed to town for the celebration, which he viewed in company with aging rancher Billy Fourr. As they discussed what was transpiring, they agreed that they did not know what the term

Helldorado meant, but from the cover design of the program and the other literature handed them they decided it meant "lurid—and alluring." Clum later wrote a small pamphlet about the event; in this he declared that the literature accompanying Helldorado Week "alleged that Tombstone, in the hectic days of its effervescent adolescence, enjoyed the dazzling reputation of being the wickedest city in this wicked old world; that its inhabitants were engaged chiefly in gambling, booze-guzzling and gun-fighting; that the final arbiter of all disputes was the six-shooter; that at least one dead man was provided for breakfast each morning; that the streets and resorts of the city presented a moving panorama of wild abandon and continuous hullabaloo performance. . . ."

He noted that he and Fourr failed to find in the presentation "any semblance of the youthful Tombstone we had known so well." In fact, wrote Clum, the two could recall only one deadly street battle and only one lynching in the fifty years of the town's existence. And in 1881, the year when most of the excitement had occurred, they recalled only six men having died violent deaths within the city's limits. Moreover, the one lynching party, that of 1884, had been organized in Bisbee, not Tombstone.[13]

The format of the celebration in 1929, little changed since, pleased the crowd that thronged to the city. Several blocks of the old business section were set apart, with two decorated arches for entrance erected on Allen Street. Twenty Yuma Indians with varying degrees of musical talent were imported to serve as the "Helldorado Band." Dressed in gaudy, feathered headbonnets (totally unknown to their ancestors) and in red shirts, they smiled and played—while their conductor occasionally used a six-shooter for a baton. The parade consisted of covered wagons, buggies, and buckboards; of women and children dressed in costumes exhumed from trunks and attics; and of cowboys and prospectors in beards, flannel shirts, high-heeled boots, and broad-brimmed hats, all carrying sufficient hardware to fight several wars. Daily there was a daring holdup of the stage coach followed by a charge of the sheriff's

Helldorado celebration, 1929. *Courtesy Arizona Historical Society.*

posse to interrupt the robbery; that would end in a heroic gun battle in which the forces of good triumphed. Another daily feature was the killing of a prospector by a drunken desperado and his prompt lynching by the righteous mob. And the Bird Cage and the Crystal Palace in the evenings resounded as of old, with skits and blackouts—and whiskey flowing briskly. Free entertainment included baton twirling, fancy shooting, boxing, wrestling, and open-air dances, while the carnival that had come to town provided sideshows, fortune telling, and bearded ladies.

The highlight of the celebration was a reenactment of the "Gunfight at the OK Corral," to which the spectators rushed. And the next day they could read the details in the *Epitaph*, which during this show became a daily once again (to revert to its weekly status when the week ended). John Clum was incensed by this reenactment: "Criminals and crime existed in Tombstone during those so-called 'hectic days' when it was a booming mining camp," he wrote. "But dissipation and disorder and lawlessness and murder were not the chief occupations of the citizens of Tombstone when

I was a resident there in the early 80's—although that impression was emphatically conveyed by the high spots in the Helldorado publicity and the Helldorado program. This is not fair simply because it is not true."[14]

Helldorado week was a success—as entertainment. The crowd went away pleased, if in ignorance as to the actual conditions that prevailed in Tombstone fifty years before. The few hundred permanent residents of the town were indeed fortunate that it had proved so, for less than a month later came a vote to move the county seat to another town in Cochise County. The residents of nearby Douglas, a copper town, had organized the move and had secured sufficient signatures on a petition to force a vote. The referendum was held on November 19, 1929, with a vote of 5926 for removal, 2724 against. Tombstone's citizens were so incensed at Douglasites for organizing the drive that they joined with the residents of Bisbee, another copper town, to have the county seat located there if it had to be moved. The vote on the new county seat, held at the same time as the referendum on moving it, resulted in 4609 votes for Bisbee, 3644 for Douglas. The official moving of the county seat took place on December 2, 1929; yet more than a year and a half elapsed before a new county courthouse, containing the necessary offices and jail, could be constructed at Bisbee. Thus it was not until April 27, 1931, that the last prisoners were removed from the Cochise County Courthouse in Tombstone.[15]

The abandoned old structure was a haunting reminder to the residents of Tombstone of the departed days of glory. In the court rooms of that structure, the walls had resounded to the eloquent oratory of some of Arizona's leading lawyers, advocates, and statesmen. For almost half a century (1881 to 1929) it had been the repository for archival records about the lives, affairs, and deaths of the people of southeastern Arizona. Yet those days were gone—never to return again. As county property, the courthouse was the responsibility of the county board of supervisors; these men on November 2, 1931, turned the building over to the city of Tombstone for fifteen years at an annual rental fee of one dollar, the city to be responsible for upkeep and necessary repairs.

A photograph of the Cochise County Court in session at Tombstone. *Courtesy Arizona Historical Society.*

Gradually the residents of Tombstone became increasingly aware of the historical significance of the old building, as well as to an appreciation of its heritage as a unique architectural structure. Thus a restoration committee was established to use the building as a museum, in the process restoring it to its original appearance and placing original furnishings in it where possible (with period furniture where the originals could not be had). The movement gained momentum, for even those citizens who did not care about historical significance or unique architecture could see that a museum might increase tourism—and thus bring money to every cash register in town. In 1955 the city of Tombstone, which by then had secured title to the building from the county, leased it to the restoration commission; then with cooperation from local citizens—and a limited budget—the commission began its work. The building was restored and opened to the public as a museum. And visitors flocked to it. But the members of the restoration committee wanted some permanent arrangement, one that would guarantee the continued operation of their handiwork. Thus they began the work that would culminate on July 1, 1959, when the old building and its contents were designated Tombstone Courthouse Historical Monument, to be operated by the State Parks Board (open from eight to five daily year around).

The courthouse might have contained original or period pieces where possible and its displays might have been carefully documented, but the rest of the town was not so authentic when the tourist boom began. And these pilgrims came, encouraged by the flood of reminiscences and enough pulp fiction to flood the city as the water beneath it had flooded the mines. Profesosr C. L. Sonnichsen, who has spent years analyzing the literature of the Southwest, once wrote that "in a class by itself as a subject for fiction is . . . Tombstone, Arizona, the most famous silver camp in the West, the number-one gunman capital, the cradle of a typically American legend: the saga of Wyatt Earp and his brothers and their friend Doc Holliday embattled against the Wild Bunch of the nearby towns and ranches." He concluded, no doubt tongue-in-cheek, that "Their Iliad and Odyssey are Walter Noble Burns' *Tombstone* and Stuart Lake's *Wyatt Earp: Frontier Marshal.*"[16]

Billy Breakenridge had started it with his *Helldorado* in 1928. When he proved there was rich ore in the stories about Tombstone's past, others followed to mine the new bonanza: Eddie Foy's *Clowning Through Life*, Lorenzo Walters' *Tombstone's Yesterday*, and several articles by John Clum. But above them all was Stuart Lake's *Wyatt Earp: Frontier Marshal*; Lake gave the public a hero, a Galahad, a virtuous American—a pasteboard character—fit to take the lead in that unique American morality play, the western. His Wyatt Earp was shy, unassuming, courteous to women, modest, violent only when forced into it, and deadly in his righteous wrath.

The first pulp fiction to use Tombstone as a setting was Alfred Henry Lewis' *Wolfville*, published in 1897; interestingly it contained no hint of the Earp legend. In the next sixteen years Lewis would publish five additional books about "Wolfville," none of which unduly represented the town. But the pulp magazines were gradually transforming the town into a wild and woolly place. Then Walter Noble Burns in 1927 produced his *Tombstone* in which he began erecting the pedestal on which Stuart Lake would place Wyatt Earp; Burns' approach, as analyzed by Professor Sonnichsen, was to make Earp Sir Galahad, his friends the Knights of the Round Table, and his enemies the wicked earls to be destroyed.[17] Gradually this fiction was refined so that in 1967, when Robert Kreps produced his *The Hour of the Gun,* virtually all proximity to the events of 1881 had been lost. Only the names are the same.[18]

And Tombstone was discovered by movie-makers. They likewise saw little commercial potential in the reality of 1881, and they, like the fictioneers, transformed the town residents into men almost evenly divided between total good and total evil. No one worked; they sat in saloons drinking and gambling and waiting to act as witnesses to the violence. They had become a lawless, brawling, eye-gouging, ear-biting breed, each with gun tied securely to thigh, ready to draw and fire with incredible speed and accuracy. One example sums up most of the movies made about Tombstone; in 1942 Paramount released an epic entitled "Tombstone, The Town Too Tough To Die," starring Richard Dix, Victor Jory, and Edgar Buchanan, which had the following inscription superimposed over the opening scenes:

> I am the voice of the past
> Of the days when I was a territory
> Overrun with bad men of all kinds
>> Rustlers
>> Dance-hall girls
>> Outlaws and gamblers
> The bad men of Arizona were strangling me with their lawlessness.
> For my existence, I am indebted to one man.
> He became a living symbol of respect for the law
> WYATT EARP.

When such books and films first began to appear, the old-timers who knew the truth laughed, realizing them to be the product of overwrought literary imaginations. But the old-timers died or else somehow remembered themselves as participants in those epic battles of yore, heroes themselves basking in reflected glory. And the money brought to Tombstone by tourists flocking to see the actual sites of those battles-for-the-right has made a new crop of believers of the more recent residents of Tombstone. Promoters have come to the city to cash in on the glories of the West that never was. Artifacts long since abandoned suddenly were transformed into "pioneer treasures" to be viewed for a fee. Pistols acquired anywhere in the West became, if not Wyatt's own handgun, at least that of Doc Holliday. The tourist pays to see a plastic replica of Tombstone in 1881.

The residents of Tombstone may be partially responsible for this distortion of the truth—for example, they still hold their annual Helldorado celebration during the week in which October 26 falls. Yet in this plastic event, they are near in spirit to the pioneers who founded the town—they are mining the only bonanza left them by the whim of fate. When the mines flooded the last time, Tombstone lost its major reason for existence, and the removal of the county seat to Bisbee left it no reason whatsoever. Thus Tombstone became almost unique among Western American cities in that it came to glory in its raw frontier beginnings. It bragged about those aspects of its past that other cities wanted forgotten. Barroom brawls, robberies, beatings, a lynching, even murder became fit subjects for street conversation and the stuff of local chroniclers. And in the process the depiction and presentation of Tombstone's history became as false as the fronts of Tombstone's stores today (and by city ordinance all new structures must be built in territorial style, thus keeping the appearance of the city similar to what it was in 1881).

The attitude of the old-timers toward this distortion of Tombstone's past was summed up by John Clum and Billy Fourr as they watched the first Helldorado celebration. Before them passed bearded men gun-fighting in the streets, prospectors staggered into town shot full of arrows, stagecoaches were robbed, and every man in sight was a walking arsenal. Fourr turned to Clum and said, "Don't you remember that away back there in 1881, when you were mayor, the men seldom grew anything but a mustache, and there was a city ordinance forbidding anyone but a peace officer to carry firearms within the city limits?"

"Well, Billy," drawled Clum in reply—and speaking for all the men who had actually built Tombstone, ". . . you must remember that *we were not giving a HELLDORADO show away back there in 1881.*"[19]

If in the grand tradition of the western book and movie there is a villain in the corruption of Tombstone's history, the bad guys are not those presenting the city as something extraordinarily lurid. It is the public which pays to see this distortion. The average tourist goes to see what he wants to believe was the past, but part of that is gone never to return and the rest never existed at all. Thus what he will view is a representation of that which is false—and in the process be separated from his money. If he is willing to pay to see a plastic replica of what he wants, even needs, the old West to have been, it is difficult to blame the people who give it to him, to say that they are wrong and he is without fault.

And the average tourist who goes to a site such as Tombstone, deny it though he may, wants to see the lurid and the violent, not the prosaic and the ordinary. There is some dark strain in the human character which attracts us to evil men and dark deeds. We identify with the man with the gun and we lust to do battle, to maim and to kill, at least vicariously; else why the emphasis on violence that is so much a part of literature, movies, and television shows? Even our heroes are capable of the most extraordinary violence—with provocation, of course, but nonetheless they are men who can kill. And their deeds become part of our folklore until the myth becomes the reality and the truth is lost. William Shakespeare some four hundred years ago recognized this quality of human nature when he had Mark Antony state, "The evil that men do lives after them, The good is oft interrèd with their bones."

Thus symbolic of the whole myth-reality of Tombstone is Boothill Cemetery, which greets the visitor as he drives into town via the Benson Highway. At that "historic" spot, when the process of sprucing up the town for the first Helldorado celebration was under

Boothill Cemetery in Tombstone, showing restored grave markers. *Courtesy Arizona Historical Society.*

way, it was discovered that most of the original cemetery had fallen into ruin; headboards were gone, and many of the graves were left unmarked. Some of the members of the restoration committee worked to check the records before new headboards were erected in order that the graves might be marked correctly, but the records were insufficiently complete to allow all of them to be identified. That did not prevent the erection of a full slate of headboards, however; some of the names on headboards, along with most of the more colorful epitaphs, were simply coined from thin air or else borrowed from other cemeteries in the West. This was the same cemetery in which the better element in the Tombstone of 1881 did not want their dead buried, and thus they started a new one for themselves. Yet today no tourist pays to see that second cemetery. It is the first—Boothill, the one filled with men who died with their boots on! And in his eagerness to see the graves of bad men and bad women, not the men and women who actually built the town and mined the ore, he is being fleeced by paying to see bogus headboards and unauthentic epitaphs.

Somehow this seems fitting. Perhaps there is a measure of justice in this world of simultaneous myth and reality.

Notes

1. For background information on this early settlement, see John L. Kessell, "The Puzzling Presidio: San Phelipe de Guevari, Alias Terrenate," *New Mexico Historical Review*, XLI (January 1966), 21-46.
2. Charles D. Poston, Tucson, *Arizona Weekly Star*, February 19, 1880; a copy is in the James B. Tenney File, Arizona Historical Society, Tucson. Hereafter the Arizona Historical Society will be cited as A.H.S.
3. "Decennial Census, 1860: Territory of New Mexico, County of Arizona," *Senate Document* 13, 89 Cong., 1 Sess., Serial 12668-1, p. 28.
4. For details of these events, see Frederick Brunckow File and James B. Tenney File, A.H.S.; *San Francisco Bulletin*, August 21, 1860; Tucson *Arizona Citizen*, June 13, 1874; Tucson *Arizona Daily Star*, July 10, 1879; Tucson *Arizona Weekly Star*, February 19, 1880; and Raphael Pumpelly, *Across America and Asia* (New York: Leypoldt and Holt, 1870).
5. "Arizona Territorial Census, 1864," *Senate Document* 13, 89 Cong., 1 Sess., Serial 12668-1, p. 58.
6. B. Sacks, "Arizona's Angry Man: United States Marshal Milton B. Duffield," Part I, *The Journal of Arizona History*, VIII (spring 1967), 1.
7. Old Book of Record B, Pima County, 88-89; Book of Mines, I, 266-68, 742-44, Pima County. See also Sacks, "Arizona's Angry Man," 115n.
8. Sacks, "Arizona's Angry Man," Part 2, *The Journal of Arizona History*, VIII (summer 1967), 112-15. On April 19, 1873, an advertisement in the Tucson *Citizen* warning against trespass had shown Mrs. Vaughn as partial owner of the mine.
9. Tucson *Arizona Daily Star*, July 10, 1879.
10. See Tucson *Arizona Weekly Star*, February 19, 1880; and the letter from Patrick Hamilton quoted in the Prescott *Arizona Democrat*, May 20, 1881.

CHAPTER 2

1. For background details on the Apache problem of southern Arizona, see Odie B. Faulk, *The Geronimo Campaign* (New York, 1969), especially pp. 11-16.

2. Ray Brandes, *Frontier Military Posts of Arizona* (Globe, Arizona: Dale Stuart King, 1960), 40.

3. The Desert Land Act of 1877, a federal law for acquiring title to public lands in the arid West, provided that a settler could obtain 640 acres if within three years he irrigated the land and made a down payment of twenty-five cents an acre; he perfected the claim and received title three years later when he was required to pay an additional one dollar per acre.

4. Patrick Hamilton, *The Resources of Arizona* (Prescott, Arizona: Under authority of the Legislature, 1881), 36.

5. James H. McClintock, *Arizona: Prehistoric, Aboriginal, Pioneer, Modern* (3 vols.; Chicago, 1916), III, 412.

6. Located in August 1874 by Jackson McCracken, this mine was employing about a hundred people by 1877. See Will C. Barnes, *Arizona Place Names* (Tucson: University of Arizona Bulletin, 1935), 258.

7. The mine and city were named for Signal Peak, from which Indians of that area had sent up smoke signals, hence the designation. The mine was on the west bank of the Big Sandy River, and was a well-known producer of the 1870s. See Barnes, *Arizona Place Names*, 407.

8. Richard Gird File, A.H.S.

9. The bulk of the information in this chapter comes from the Ed Schieffelin File, A.H.S., and from Schieffelin's "History of the Discovery of Tomstone, Arizona, as told by the Discoverer, Edward Schieffelin." A copy of this manuscript is in the Arizona Historical Society; Schieffelin wrote this at the request of historian Hubert Howe Bancroft. See also John Vosburg File, A.H.S., for additional details.

CHAPTER 3

1. Later James would work at the Contention Mine as a surveyor and drafts-man. See W. P. Blake, *Tombstone and Its Mines* (New York: Cheltenham Press, 1902), 75.

2. Tucson *Arizona Daily Star*, September 19, 1879.

3. Richard W. Fulton, "Millville-Charleston, Cochise County, 1879-1889," *The Journal of Arizona History*, VII (spring 1966), 10.

4. For an excellent description of Western miners and their methods of work, see Otis E. Young, Jr., *Western Mining: An Informal Account of Precious-Metals Prospecting, Placering, Lode Mining, and Milling on the American*

Frontier from Spanish Times to 1893 (Norman: University of Oklahoma Press, 1970), particularly pages 178-91.

5. David Pitts Reminiscence, in Mrs. Anna J. Emmons File, A.H.S.
6. Jacob H. Marcus (ed.), "An Arizona Memoir of Sam Aaron," *American Jewish Archives*, X (October 1958), 106.
7. "Personal Recollections of John Vosburg to Frank Lockwood at Tombstone," Lockwood Collection, A.H.S.; Vosburg File, A.H.S.; and Schieffelin File, A.H.S. There are some differences between Schieffelin's reminiscences of the events that spring and summer of 1878 and those of Vosburg. Especially noticeable is Vosburg's claim that he was approached for grubstaking by the Schieffelins and Gird before the three ever journeyed to the Tombstone area together. I have followed each reminiscence in part, relying on the one best substantiated by other sources when they diverge.
8. Tucson *Arizona Daily Star*, June 26, 1879.
9. Schieffelin File, A.H.S.
10. Interview of Rockfellow by Alice Emily Love, cited in her "The History of Tombstone to 1887" (unpublished master's thesis, the University of Arizona, 1933), 19.
11. Hamilton, *Resources of Arizona*, 36.
12. *Ibid.*, edition of 1883, 76-77.
13. *Ibid.*, 75; Blake, *Tombstone and Its Mines*, 63.
14. Blake, *Tombstone and Its Mines*, 61.

CHAPTER 4

1. Barnes, *Arizona Place Names*, 88.
2. See Books I, II, and III, Recorder's Office, Cochise County Courthouse, Bisbee, Arizona. Two excellent articles reconstruct Charleston's early years: Fulton, "Millville-Charleston," and Richard W. Fulton and Conrad J. Bahre (eds.), "Charleston, Arizona: A Documentary Reconstruction," *Arizona and the West*, IX (spring 1967), 41-64.
3. Barnes, *Arizona Place Names*, 150.
4. *Ibid.*, 108.
5. *Ibid.*, 172.
6. *Ibid.*, 477.
7. Byrd H. Granger, *Will C. Barnes' Arizona Place Names* (Tucson: University of Arizona Press, 1960), 54-55.
8. Tucson *Arizona Daily Star*, November 11, 1880.
9. Quoted in J. Hayes, "Tomsbtone Town-site" (unpublished brief, 1882; copy in A.H.S.).
10. Tucson *Arizona Weekly Star*, November 1 and December 9, 1879.

11. Lucius Nutting Reminiscence, in Margaret Bayless Smallhouse File, A.H.S.

12. McClintock, *Arizona*, II, 582.

13. Quoted in Joseph Miller, *Arizona: The Last Frontier* (New York, 1956), 129.

14. John Pleasant Gray Reminiscence, A.H.S.

15. Quoted in Thomas Peterson, "Sandy Bob and Others" (unpublished seminar paper, University of Arizona, 1964).

16. Gray Reminiscence, A.H.S.

17. David F. Myrick, "The Railroads of Southern Arizona: An Approach to Tombstone," *The Journal of Arizona History*, VIII (autumn 1967), 155-70.

18. Parsons *Journal*, 92.

19. *Statistics of the Population of the United States at the 10th Census (June 1, 1880)*, Washington, 1883, I, 99.

20. *Ibid.*, 47.

21. McClintock, *Arizona*, II, 332.

22. *Acts and Resolutions of the Eleventh Legislative Assembly of the Territory of Arizona* (Prescott: Office of the Arizona Miner, 1881), 98, 101, 108, 169.

23. *Ibid.*, 37-38.

24. See George H. Kelly, *Legislative History, Arizona, 1864-1912* (Phoenix: Office of the State Historian, 1926), 96-98, which quotes the San Francisco *Bulletin*.

25. Mrs. Aura H. Gordon File, A.H.S.

26. Hal Dickey, *The Famous Crystal Palace* (pamphlet, n.p., n.d.).

27. For details, see Pat M. Ryan, "John P. Clum: 'Boss-With-the-White-Forehead,'" *Arizoniana*, V (fall 1964), 48-58; and Ryan, "Trail-Blazer of Civilization: John P. Clum's Tucson and Tombstone Years," *The Journal of Arizona History*, VI (summer 1965), 53-70. For details about the *Epitaph*, see Douglas D. Martin, *Tombstone's Epitaph* (Albuquerque: University of New Mexico Press, 1951).

28. Goodfellow File, A.H.S., and Thomas E. Gibson, "George E. Goodfellow," *Surgery, Gynecology, and Obstetrics*, LIV (April 1932), 716-18.

29. J. Rowland Hill, "Arizona's Development," *The Golden Era*, XXXVIII (May 1889), 198.

30. *Ibid.*, 202-3; Blake, *Tombstone and Its Mines*, 23.

31. Gray Reminiscence, A.H.S.

CHAPTER 5

1. Gray Reminiscence, A.H.S.

2. Parsons, *Journal*, 92, 94, 100.

3. Ordinance No. 39, City of Tombstone, published on March 17, 1882.

4. Parsons, *Journal*, 98.

5. *Ibid.*, 94, 100, 102, 107-8.

6. *Ibid.*, 100.

7. James G. Wolf File, A.H.S.

8. Parsons, *Journal*, 142-143; Tombstone *Epitaph*, September 1, 1880.

9. Jerry Wallace, "How the Episcopal Church Came to Arizona," *The Journal of Arizona History*, VI (autumn 1965), 111.

10. Odie B. Faulk (ed.), *John Baptist Salpointe: Soldier of the Cross* (Tucson: Diocese of Tucson, 1966), 134-35; Salpointe File, A.H.S.

11. James G. Wolf Reminiscence, A.H.S.

12. J. C. Hancock Memoirs, in Frank Lockwood Collection, A.H.S.

13. *Ibid.*

14. Collections of such photographs have survived, but for obvious reasons the historical societies which own them do not have them catalogued.

15. James G. Wolf in his reminiscence left an excellent description of this process. Rumors, along with some strong documentary evidence, suggest that these prostitutes following the army paymasters around Arizona were financed by the bankers of Tucson and other frontier cities.

16. Wolf Reminiscence, A.H.S.

17. Edith M. Stowe Reminiscence, A.H.S.

18. John M. Myers, *The Last Chance: Tombstone's Early Years* (New York, 1951), 51.

19. Hill, "Arizona's Development," 204-5.

20. *Tombstone Prospector*, February 9, 1888.

21. Tombstone *Epitaph*, November 17, 1881.

22. "Introduction" in Hamilton, *Resources of Arizona* (reprint of 1881 original; Tucson: Piñon Press, 1966).

23. Charles Andress, a magician, recalled this incident, which was published in the Tucson *Arizona Star*, May 8, 1930.

24. Tombstone *Epitaph*, November 30, 1880.

25. Tucson *Arizona Star*, March 31, 1881.

26. For additional details about the theater and theatricals in Tombstone, see Pat M. Ryan's excellent "Tombstone Theatre Tonight!" *The Smoke Signal*, XIII (spring 1966), 49-76.

27. Wolf Reminiscence, A.H.S.

28. Gray Reminiscence, A.H.S.

29. Wolf Reminiscence, A.H.S.

30. Gray Reminiscence, A.H.S.

31. David Pitts Reminiscence, in Mrs. Anna J. Emmons File, A.H.S.

CHAPTER 6

1. Copy in Aura G. Gordon File, A.H.S.
2. Gray Reminiscence, A.H.S.
3. Henry P. Walker, "Retire Peacefully to Your Homes: Arizona Faces Martial Law, 1882," *The Journal of Arizona History*, X (spring 1969), 7.
4. *Ibid.*, 9-14. See also Gary L. Roberts, "The 'Cow-Boy Scourge,'" New York Posse *Westerners' Brand Book*, IX (No. 2, 1962), 28-29, 36-37.
5. James D. Richardson (comp.), *A Compilation of the Messages and Papers of the Presidents* (20 vols.; New York, 1897), X, 4640-41.
6. John P. Clum Manuscript (typescript copy in Division of Special Collections, Library, University of Arizona, Tucson).
7. For his account of these events, written in almost fictionalized form, see William Breakenridge, *Helldorado* (Boston, 1929).
8. Gray Reminiscence, A.H.S.; and Ryan, "Trail-Blazer of Civilization," 66.
9. Tucson *Arizona Daily Star*, June 23, 1881.
10. Stacy Osgood, "The Life and Times of David Neagle," Chicago *Westerners' Brand Book*, XIX (April 1962), n.p.; Frank Waters, *The Earp Brothers of Tombstone* (New York, 1960), 139-41.
11. Waters, *The Earp Brothers of Tombstone*, 110-12.
12. Tombstone *Epitaph*, March 12, 1931.
13. Gray Reminiscence, A.H.S.
14. Tombstone *Epitaph*, March 12, 1931.
15. Cochise County Records. Coroner—Bills for Inquests, 1881-1883 (dated November 8, 1881), A.H.S.
16. Parsons, *Journal*, 270-71.
17. Tombstone *Epitaph*, December 18, 1881.
18. John P. Clum, "It All Happened in Tombstone," *Arizona Historical Review*, II (April 1929), 56-62. This same article, edited and annotated by John Gilchriese, appeared in *Arizona and the West*, II (spring 1960), and later was reprinted as a book, *It All Happened in Tombstone* (Flagstaff: Northland Press, 1963).
19. For Wyatt Earp's version of this affair, see Stuart N. Lake, *Wyatt Earp: Frontier Marshal* (New York, 1931), 319-24.
20. Osgood, "Life and Times of David Neagle."
21. *Ibid.*
22. Walker, "Retire Peacefully to Your Homes," 5-6.
23. Richardson (comp.), *Messages and Papers of the Presidents*, X, 4688-89.
24. Tombstone *Epitaph*, May 13, 1882. There are so many conflicting accounts of the Earps in Tombstone that no one book will give a complete picture of the bloody events of that time. I personally believe the best

account to be Frank Waters, *The Earp Brothers of Tombstone,* although pro-
and anti-Earp books abound. The reader can easily find something to sus-
tain whatever he believes. I have not cited here, but include in the bibliography, a dozen and more books which relate in large measure to the contents
of this chapter.

25. Goodfellow File, A.H.S., and John Heath File, A.H.S.

CHAPTER 7

1. Thomas Carson, *Ranching, Sport and Travel* (London: F. Fisher Unwin, 1911, and New York, 1912), 68-69.
2. Schieffelin Reminiscence, A.H.S.; and Tucson *Arizona Weekly Star,* March 18, 1880.
3. Tombstone *Epitaph,* January 12, 1882; see also Jay J. Wagoner, *Arizona Territory, 1863-1912: A Political History* (Tucson: University of Arizona Press, 1970), 118.
4. Vosburg Reminiscence, A.H.S.
5. *Ibid.*
6. Gird File, A.H.S.; Tucson *Arizona Weekly Star,* September 30, 1880; Phoenix *Herald,* May 27, 1881.
7. Gird File, A.H.S.; Schieffelin File, A.H.S. See also Devere, "The Tombstone Bonanza," 19.
8. Quoted in Frank Lockwood, *Pioneer Portraits: Selected Vignettes* (Tucson: University of Arizona Press, 1968), 188-89.
9. Tucson *Arizona Weekly Star,* May 15, 1884.
10. *Ibid.*
11. Hamilton, *Resources of Arizona* (1884 edition), 156.
12. Blake, *Tombstone and Its Mines,* 17.
13. Fulton and Bahre, "Charleston, Arizona," 61.
14. Tombstone *Prospector,* June 14, 1889.
15. Quoted in Martin, *Tombstone's Epitaph,* 257-58.
16. *Ibid.,* 258-59.
17. Hill, "Arizona's Development," 201. See also Blake, *Tombstone and Its Mines,* 18, which quotes a letter by W. F. Stanton dated June 19, 1901, to the Development Company of America (pp. 16-18).
18. Hill, "Arizona's Development," 202.
19. For details of the Apache wars, see Faulk, *The Geronimo Campaign.*
20. For a good history of this development, see Jay J. Wagoner, *The History of the Cattle Industry in Southern Arizona, 1540-1940* (Tucson: University of Arizona Bulletin, 1952).
21. For Slaughter's career, see Allen A. Erwin, *The Southwest of John H.*

Slaughter, 1841-1922 (Glendale, California: Arthur H. Clark Company, 1965), especially Chapter 8.

22. Quoted in Martin, *Tombstone's Epitaph*, 259.

23. Blake, *Tombstone and Its Mines*, 19.

24. Tombstone *Epitaph*, November 22, 1902.

25. Tombstone *Epitaph*, February 2, 1903.

26. Young, *Western Mining*, 279; Martin, *Tombstone's Epitaph*, Chapter 13, especially 271-72.

CHAPTER 8

1. Quoted in Erwin, *The Southwest of John H. Slaughter*, 181.

2. Quoted in Lockwood, *Pioneer Portraits: Selected Vignettes*, 189; see also Erwin, *The Southwest of John H. Slaughter*, 182-83.

3. Gird File, A.H.S.

4. Clum File, A.H.S. For a biographical sketch, plus bibliography of Clum's writings, see Pat M. Ryan, "John P. Clum: Boss-With-the-White-Forehead," *Arizoniana*, V (fall 1964), 48-60.

5. See Waters, *The Earps of Tombstone*, 217-19. This is without doubt the best book yet written about the Earps; many of the other books on them might be mentioned only for purposes of humor.

6. The extent of Wyatt Earp's personal contribution to this book is debatable; see Glenn G. Boyer, *The Suppressed Murder of Wyatt Earp* (San Antonio: Naylor Company, 1967).

7. C. L. Sonnichsen, *Billy King's Tombstone: The Private Life of an Arizona Boom Town* (Caldwell, Idaho: Caxton Printers, 1942), 164-65.

8. Lloyd and Rose Hamill, *Tombstone Picture Gallery* (Glendale, California: Western Americana Press, 1960), 8.

9. Sonnichsen, *Billy King's Tombstone*, 182-83.

10. *Ibid.*, 95-98.

11. *Ibid.*, 113-15. For another view of the Chinese contribution to Tombstone, see H. H. Niemeyer, "Quong Kee of Tombstone," *St. Louis Post Dispatch*, Sunday Magazine, March 13, 1938.

12. John P. Clum, "Nellie Cashman," *Arizona Historical Review*, III (January 1931), 9-34.

13. John P. Clum, *Helldorado, 1879-1929* (pamphlet, n.p., n.d.), 4-9.

14. John P. Clum, "Tombstone's Semi-Centennial," *Arizona Historical Review*, II (January 1930), 28-30.

15. All major Arizona newspapers carried stories about this vote and the movement of the prisoners; for details, see the newspaper on the relevant date.

16. C. L. Sonnichsen, "Tombstone in Fiction," *The Journal of Arizona History,* IX (summer 1968), 59. See also Sonnichsen, "The Wyatt Earp Syndrome," *The American West,* VII (May 1970), 26-28, 60-62.

17. Sonnichsen, "Tombstone in Fiction," 62.

18. *Ibid.,* 74-75.

19. Clum, *Helldorado, 1879-1929,* 9.

Bibliography

Samuel Eliot Morison in his recent *The European Discovery of America: The Northern Voyages, A.D. 500-1600* (New York, 1971) stated in his Preface, ". . . It has fallen to my lot, working on this subject, to have read some of the most tiresome historical literature in existence. . . . In my bibliographies I have included a few of these articles for the unconscious humor they provide . . ." (pp. vii-viii). I would add to this that it also has fallen to my lot, while working on the subject of Tombstone, to have read some of the finest books in existence along with some of the worst. Tombstone is a subject that has generated both strong positive and negative passions. Thus the reader interested in pursuing the subject will find something among the following materials to fit any preconceived notions he may hold, or, if he is interested in the truth, enough to give him material for thought for some time.

MANUSCRIPT SOURCES

Arizona Historical Society, Tucson. This institution, the state historical society for Arizona, has biographical files on most of the participants in this story. Hereafter cited as A.H.S.
Frederick Brunckow File, A.H.S.
John Clum File, A.H.S.
John P. Clum Manuscript. Copy in the Division of Special Collections, Library, University of Arizona, Tucson.
Cochise County Records, Bisbee, Arizona.

222   *Bibliography*

Cochise County Records, Coroner's File, A.H.S.
Mrs. Anna J. Emmons File, A.H.S.
Richard Gird File, A.H.S.
George Goodfellow File, A.H.S.
Mrs. Aura H. Gordon File, A.H.S.
John Pleasant Gray Reminiscence, A.H.S.
J. Hayes, "Tombstone Town-Site," unpublished brief, 1882; copy in
    A.H.S.
John Heath File, A.H.S.
Frank Lockwood Collection, A.H.S.
Alice E. Love, "The History of Tombstone to 1887" (unpublished
    master's thesis, University of Arizona, 1933).
Thomas Peterson, "Sandy Bob and Others" (unpublished seminar
    paper, University of Arizona, 1964).
Pima County Book of Mines, County Courthouse, Tucson.
Ed Schieffelin File, A.H.S.
Ed Schieffelin, "History of the Discovery of Tombstone, Arizona, as
    told by the Discoverer, Edward Schieffelin," manuscript copy
    in A.H.S.
Margaret Bayless Smallhouse File, A.H.S.
Edith M. Stowe Reminiscence, A.H.S.
James B. Tenney File, A.H.S.
John Vosburg File, A.H.S.
James G. Wolf Reminiscence, A.H.S.

NEWSPAPERS

There were ten newspapers published in Tombstone during the years
covered by this study; for a complete listing of these, along with their
editors, publishers, and dates, see Estelle Lutrell, *Newspapers and
Periodicals of Arizona, 1895-1911* (Tucson: University of Arizona
Bulletin, 1949).

Chicago *Daily Tribune*
Phoenix Herald
San Francisco Bulletin
San Francisco *Mining and Scientific Press*
St. Louis Post Dispatch
Prescott *Arizona Democrat*

Tombstone *Epitaph*
Tombstone *Independent*
Tombstone *Daily Nugget*
Tucson *Arizona Daily Star* (also published as the *Star, Weekly Star,* and *Arizona Star*)
Tucson *Daily Citizen* (also published as the *Citizen, Arizona Citizen,* and *Weekly Citizen*)

BOOKS

Acts and Resolutions of the Eleventh Legislative Assembly of the Territory of Arizona. Prescott: Office of the Arizona Miner, 1881.

Andrews, Ralph W. *Photographs of the Frontier West.* Seattle: Superior, 1965.

Bakarich, Sarah Grace. *Gun-Smoke.* N.P.: privately printed, 1947.

Barnes, Will C. *Arizona Place Names.* Tucson: University of Arizona Bulletin, 1935.

Bartholomew, Ed Ellsworth. *Wyatt Earp, 1848 to 1880: The Untold Story.* Toyahvale, Texas: Frontier Book Company, 1963.

———. *Wyatt Earp, 1879 to 1882: The Man and the Myth.* Toyahvale, Texas: Frontier Book Company, 1964.

Bechdolt, Frederick W. *When the West Was Young.* New York, 1922.

Bishop, William H. *Old Mexico and Her Lost Provinces: A Journey Through Mexico.* New York, 1887.

Blake, William Phipps. *Tombstone and Its Mines: A Report Upon the Past and Present Condition of the Mines of Tombstone, Cochise County, Arizona.* New York: Cheltenham Press, 1902.

Brandes, Ray. *Frontier Military Posts of Arizona.* Globe, Arizona: Dale Stuart King, 1960.

Breakenridge, William M. *Helldorado.* Boston, 1928.

Briggs, L. Vernon. *Arizona and New Mexico in 1882, California in 1886, Mexico 1891.* Boston: privately printed, 1932 (and reprint).

Boyer, Glenn G. *The Suppressed Murder of Wyatt Earp.* San Antonio: Naylor, 1967.

Burgess, Opie Rundle. *Bisbee Not So Long Ago.* San Antonio: Naylor, 1967.

Burnham, Frederick R. *Scouting on Two Continents.* Garden City, New York, 1926.

Burns, Walter N. *Tombstone: An Iliad of the Southwest.* Garden City, New York, 1927.

Carson, Thomas. *Ranching, Sport and Travel.* London, 1911, and New York, 1912.

Clum, John P. *Helldorado, 1879-1929.* N.p., n.d. (pamphlet).

―――. *It All Happened in Tombstone,* ed. by John Gilchriese. Flagstaff, Arizona: Northland Press, 1965.

Clum, Woodworth. *Apache Agent: The Story of John Clum.* Boston, 1936.

Coolidge, Dane. *Fighting Men of the West.* New York, 1932.

Cunningham, Eugene. *Triggernometry.* Caldwell, Idaho: Caxton Printers, 1936.

Dickey, Hal. *The Famous Crystal Palace.* N.p., n.d. (pamphlet).

Erwin, Allen A. *The Southwest of John H. Slaughter, 1841-1922.* Glendale, California: Arthur H. Clark, 1965.

Faulk, Odie B. *The Geronimo Campaign.* New York, 1969.

――― (ed.). *John Baptist Salpointe: Soldier of the Cross.* Tucson: Diocese of Tucson, 1966.

Franke, Paul. *They Plowed Up Hell in Old Cochise.* Douglas, Arizona: Douglas Climate Club, 1950.

Ganzhorn, Jack, *I've Killed Men.* London, and New York, 1954.

Granger, Byrd H. *Will C. Barnes' Arizona Place Names.* Tucson: University of Arizona Press, 1960.

Hall-Quest, Olga W. *Wyatt Earp: Marshall of the Old West.* New York, 1956.

Hamilton, Patrick. *The Resources of Arizona.* Prescott, Arizona: Under Authority of the Legislature, 1881 (this was the second edition of this book; the first was printed at Florence, Arizona, in 1881; the third edition would be in San Francisco: A. L. Bancroft, 1883, and revised again in 1884).

Hamill, Lloyd and Rose. *Tombstone Picture Gallery.* Glendale, California: Western Americana Press, 1960.

Hattich, William. *Pioneer Magic.* New York, 1964.

Hayden, Ward. *Tombstone Tragedies and Triumphs.* New York, 1966.

Hogan, Ray. *Johnny Ringo: Gentleman Outlaw.* London: J. Long, 1964.

Hughes, Dan de Lara. *South from Tombstone*. London: Methuen and Company, 1938.

Hunter, John M., and Noah H. Rose. *The Album of Gun Fighters*. Bandera, Texas: privately printed, 1951.

Jaastad, Ben. *Man of the West*. Tucson: Arizona Pioneers' Historical Society, 1956.

Jahns, Pat. *The Frontier World of Doc Holliday*. New York, 1957.

Kelly, George H. *Legislative History, Arizona, 1864-1912*. Phoenix: Office of the State Historian, 1926.

Lake, Carolyn (ed.). *Under Cover for Wells Fargo*. Boston, 1969.

Lake, Stuart N. *Wyatt Earp: Frontier Marshal*. Boston, 1931.

Lakes, Arthur. *Prospecting for Gold and Silver in North America*. 2nd edition. Scranton, 1896.

Lewis, Alfred H. *Wolfville*. New York, 1897 (fiction).

Lockwood, Frank. *Pioneer Days in Arizona*. New York, 1932.

———. *Pioneer Portraits: Selected Vignettes*. Tucson: University of Arizona Press, 1968.

McClintock, James H. *Arizona: Prehistoric, Aboriginal, Pioneer, Modern*. 3 vols. Chicago: S. J. Clark Company, 1916.

Martin, Douglas D. *The Earps of Tombstone*. Tombstone: Tombstone Epitaph, 1959 (pamphlet).

———. *Silver, Sex, and Six Guns: Tombstone Saga of the Life of Buckskin Frank Leslie*. Tombstone: Tombstone Epitaph, 1962 (pamphlet).

———. *Tombstone's Epitaph*. Albuquerque: University of New Mexico Press, 1951.

Miller, Joseph. *Arizona: The Last Frontier*. New York, 1956.

Myers, John M. *Doc Holliday*. Boston, 1955.

———. *The Last Chance: Tombstone's Early Years*. New York, 1951.

Nunnelley, Lela S. *Boothill Grave Yard*. Tombstone: Tombstone Press, 1952 (pamphlet).

Olsson, Jan Olof, *Welcome to Tombstone*. London: Elek Books, 1956.

Parsons, George W. *The Private Journal of George Whitwell Parsons*. Phoenix: W.P.A., 1939 (mimeograph).

Poston, Charles D. *Building a State in Apache Land*. Tempe, Arizona: Aztec Press, 1963 (originally published in *Overland Monthly*, XXIV, 2nd Series, 1894).

Pumpelly, Raphael. *Across America and Asia*. New York, 1870.

Raine, William McLeod. *Famous Sheriffs and Western Outlaws.* Garden City, New York, 1929.

———. *45-Caliber Law: The Way of the Frontier Peace Officer.* Evanston, Illinois: Row-Peterson Unitext, 1941.

Richardson, James D. (comp.). *A Compilation of the Messages and Papers of the Presidents.* 20 vols. New York, 1897.

Rosa, Joseph G. *The Gunfighter: Man or Myth?* Norman: University of Oklahoma Press, 1969.

Sonnichsen, C. L. *Billy King's Tombstone: The Private Life of an Arizona Boom Town.* Caldwell, Idaho: Caxton Printers, 1942.

Statistics of the Population of the United States at the 10th Census. Washington, 1883.

Tilghman, Zoe A. *Spotlight: Bat Masterson and Wyatt Earp as U. S. Marshals.* San Antonio: Naylor, 1960.

Wagoner, J. J. *Arizona Territory, 1863-1912: A Political History.* Tucson: University of Arizona Press, 1970.

———. *The History of the Cattle Industry in Southern Arizona, 1540-1940.* Tucson: University of Arizona Bulletin, 1952.

Walters, Lorenzo D. *Tombstone's Yesterdays.* Tucson: Acme Printing Co., 1928 (and reprint).

Waters, Frank. *The Earp Brothers of Tombstone.* New York, 1960.

Welles, A. M. *Reminiscent Ramblings.* Denver: The W. F. Robinson Printing Company, 1905.

Wench, Harold Edgar. *Phantoms of Old Tombstone.* Tucson: Arizona Silhouettes, 1951.

White, Edward P. *Ballads of Tombstone's Yesterdays, by Ned White.* Bisbee: Press of F. A. McKinney, 1929.

Willson, Claire Eugene. *Mimes and Miners: An Historical Study of the Theater in Tombstone.* Tucson: University of Arizona Bulletin, 1935.

Young, Otis E., Jr. *Western Mining: An Informal Account of Precious-Metals, Prospecting, Placering, Lode Mining, and Milling on the American Frontier From Spanish Times to 1893.* Norman: University of Oklahoma Press, 1970.

ARTICLES

Alderson, Nova. "Frontier Literature: or, A Fast Draw on Navajo Nick,

Tombstone Tom and Arizona Charlie," *Arizoniana*, II (summer 1961), 27-31.

"Arizona Territorial Census, 1864," *Senate Document* 13, 89 Cong., 1 Sess., Serial 12668-1.

Baumgart, Edward J. (ed.). "An Evaluation of Banking in Arizona," *Arizoniana*, III (winter 1962), 45-48.

Brimmer, Leonora. "Boothill Graveyard," *Arizona Highways*, XXIV (January 1948), 12-17.

Clum, John P. "It All Happened in Tombstone," *Arizona Historical Review*, II (April 1929), 46-72 (reprinted in *Arizona and the West*, II, spring 1960, edited by John Gilchriese; see also its listing as a book).

————. "Nellie Cashman," *Arizona Historical Review*, III (January 1931), 9-34.

————. "Tombstone's Semi-Centennial," *Arizona Historical Review*, II (January 1930), 28-30.

Comfort, Will L. "Tombstone and Its Epitaph," *Saturday Evening Post* (April 26, 1930), 12-13, 85-90.

Cubley, Clark A., and Joseph A. Steiner, "Emilio Kosterlitzsky," *Arizoniana*, I (winter 1960), 12-14.

"Decennial Census, 1860: Territory of New Mexico, County of Arizona," *Senate Document* 13, 89 Cong., 1 Sess., Serial 12668-1.

Devere, Jeanne, "The Tombstone Bonanza, 1878-1886," *Arizoniana*, I (fall 1960), 16-20.

Duffen, William A. "Notes on the Earp-Clanton Feud," *Arizoniana*, I (fall 1960), 20-22.

Forrest, Earle R. "The Fabulous Sierra Bonita," *The Journal of Arizona History*, VI (autumn 1965), 132-46.

Fulton, Richard W. "Millville-Charleston, Cochise County, 1879-1889," *The Journal of Arizona History*, VII (spring 1966), 9-22.

————, and Conrad J. Bahre (eds.). "Charleston, Arizona: A Documentary Reconstruction," *Arizona and the West*, IX (spring 1967), 41-64.

Gibson, Thomas E. "George E. Goodfellow," *Surgery, Gynecology, and Obstetrics*, LIX (April 1932), 716-18.

Gregg, Mike. "Uncle Billy Fourr: Cattleman Extraordinaire," *Arizoniana*, II (fall 1961), 20-24.

Gregory, Leslie E. "John P. Clum," *Arizona Historical Review*, V (July 1932), 89-94, and (October 1932), 188-97.

Hattich, William. "Highlights on Arizona's First Printing Press," *Arizona Historical Review*, III (October 1930), 67-72.

Hill, Gertrude. "Henry Clay Hooker: King of the Sierra Bonita," *Arizoniana*, II (winter 1961), 12-15.

Hill, J. Rowland. "Arizona's Development," *The Golden Era*, XXXVIII (May 1889), 195-207.

Kellner, Larry. "William Milton Breakenridge: Deadliest Two-Gun Deputy of Arizona," *Arizoniana*, II (winter 1961), 20-22.

Kessell, John L. "The Puzzling Presidio: San Phelipe de Guevavi, Alias Terrenate," *New Mexico Historical Review*, XLI (January 1966), 21-46.

Kitt, Mrs. George F. (ed.). "Reminiscences of William Fourr," *Arizona Historical Review*, VI (October 1935), 68-84.

Loomis, Noel M. "Early Cattle Trails in Southern Arizona," *Arizoniana*, III (winter 1962), 18-24.

Lutrell, Estelle. "Arizona's Frontier Press," *Arizona Historical Review*, VI (January 1935), 14-27.

Marcus, Jacob R. (ed.). "An Arizona Memoir of Sam Aaron," *American Jewish Archives*, X (October 1958), 95-120.

Miller, Joseph. "Tombstone, 'The Town Too Tough To Die,' " *Arizona Highways*, XXI (May 1945), 32-37.

"The Mills in Tombstone District," *Arizona Quarterly Illustrated*, I (October 1880), 15.

Myrick, David F. "The Railroads of Southern Arizona: An Approach to Tombstone," *The Journal of Arizona History*, VIII (autumn 1967), 155-170.

Niemeyer, H. H. "Quong Kee of Tombstone," *St. Louis Post Dispatch* Sunday Magazine, March 13, 1938.

Osgood, Stacy. "The Life and Times of David Neagle," Chicago *Westerners' Brand Book*, XIX (April 1962), n.p.

Rickards, Colin. "Buckskin Frank Leslie: Gunman of Tombstone," *Southwestern Studies*, II (summer 1964), 1-39.

Roberts, Gary L. "The Cow-Boy Scourge," New York Posse *Westerners' Brand Book*, IX (No. 2, 1962), 28-29, 36-37.

———. "The Wells Spicer Decision: 1881," *Montana*, XX (winter 1970), 62-74.

————. "The West's Gunmen: I, The Historiography of the Frontier Heroes," *The American West,* VIII (January 1971), 10-15, 64.

————. "The West's Gunmen: II, Recent Historiography of Those Controversial Heroes," *The American West,* VIII (March 1971), 18-23, 61-62.

Ryan, Pat M. "John P. Clum: 'Boss-with-the-White-Forehead,' " *Arizoniana,* V (fall 1964), 48-60.

————. "Tombstone Theatre Tonight," *The Smoke Signal,* XIII (spring 1966), 49-76.

————. "Trail-Blazer of Civilization: John P. Clum's Tucson and Tombstone Years," *The Journal of Arizona History,* VI (summer 1965), 53-70.

Sacks, B. "Arizona's Angry Man: United States Marshal Milton B. Duffield," *The Journal of Arizona History,* VIII (spring 1967), 1-29, and (summer 1967), 91-119.

Seligmann, G. L. "Crawley P. Dake: U. S. Marshal," *Arizoniana,* II (spring 1961), 13-14.

Serven, James E. "The Gun—An Instrument of Destiny in Arizona," *Arizoniana,* V (fall 1964), 14-28.

Sonnichsen, C. L. "Tombstone in Fiction," *The Journal of Arizona History,* IX (summer 1968), 58-76.

————. "The Wyatt Earp Syndrome," *The American West,* VII (May 1970), 26-28, 60-62.

"Tombstone District Developments," *Arizona Quarterly Illustrated,* I (July 1880), 3.

Wagoner, J. J. "Overstocking of the Ranges in Southern Arizona During the 1870's and 1880's," *Arizoniana,* II (spring 1961), 23-27.

Walker, Elton W. "Sinking a Wet Shaft at Tombstone," *Mining and Scientific Press,* XCVIII (February 20, 1909), 284-86.

Walker, Henry P. "Retire Peaceably to Your Homes: Arizona Faces Martial Law, 1882," *The Journal of Arizona History,* X (spring 1969), 1-18.

Wallace, Jerry. "How the Episcopal Church Came to Arizona," *The Journal of Arizona History,* VI (autumn 1965), 101-15.

Wehrman, Georgia. "Harshaw: Mining Camp of the Patagonias," *The Journal of Arizona History,* VI (spring 1965), 21-36.

Index

231